THE BELLCREST SERIES

English for Business

OXFORD UNIVERSITY PRESS

Oxford University Press, Walton Street, Oxford OX2 6DP
LONDON GLASGOW NEW YORK TORONTO
DELHI BOMBAY CALCUTTA MADRAS KARACHI
KUALA LUMPUR SINGAPORE HONG KONG TOKYO
NAIROBI DAR ES SALAAM CAPE TOWN SALISBURY
MELBOURNE AUCKLAND

and associates in
BEIRUT BERLIN IBADAN MEXICO CITY NICOSIA

ISBN 0 19 457110 6 (Student's Book)

First published 1973
Seventh impression 1982

English for Business was researched, developed and written by the Oxford University Press English Language Teaching Development Unit and produced in association with the BBC and the British Council.

Illustrations by Geoffrey Bargery

Printed in Hong Kong

CONTENTS

THE STRUCTURE OF BELLCREST LIMITED

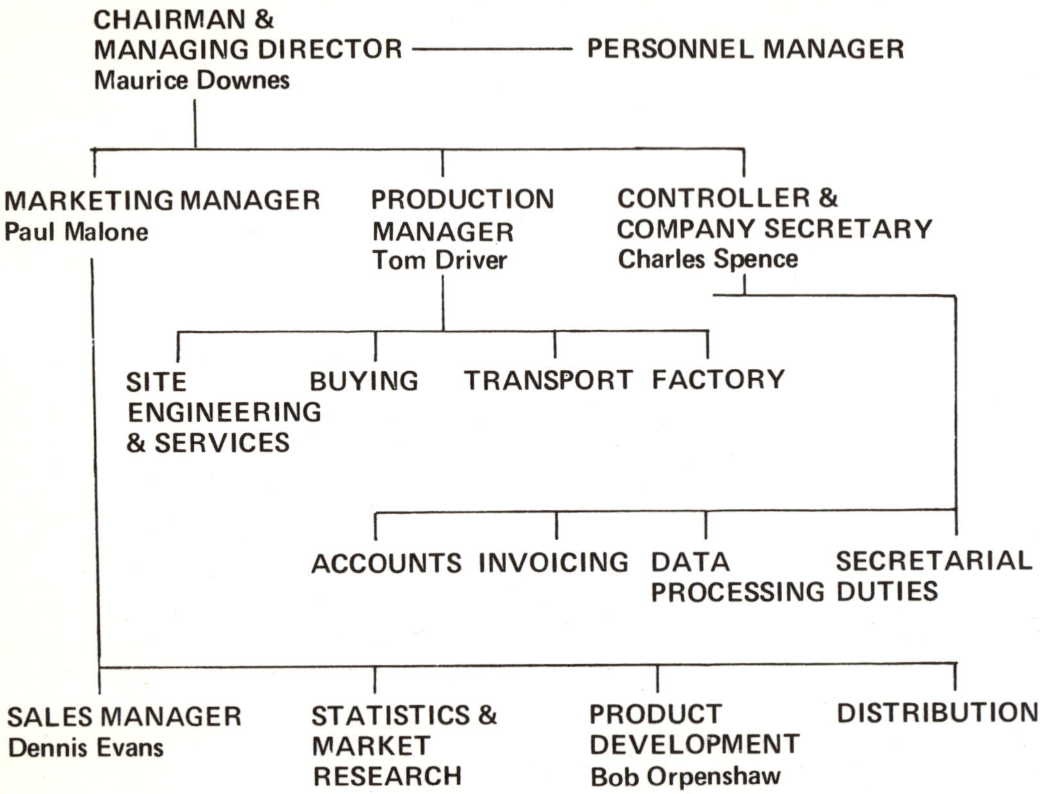

DIVERSIFICATION

George Hanson, a journalist writing a series of articles on successful companies, visited Bellcrest to make a case study of the firm. Bellcrest Limited is a medium sized company with its factory and offices near Leicester in the English Midlands. It manufactures electronic components for computers and communications and control systems.

Hanson learned that five years ago Bellcrest was in financial difficulties, because it had been concentrating on the research and development of new products rather than on marketing them. Ashburnham's, the merchant bank, made a loan of £300,000, at a low rate of interest, and bought a percentage of the shares. They put Edward Needham, Sir Frederick Ashburnham's assistant, on the Board of Directors and appointed Maurice Downes as Chairman and Managing Director.

As Downes and the Marketing Manager, Donald Williams, disagreed on policy over discontinuing certain products; Williams was forced to resign and Downes appointed Paul Malone in his place. Downes reduced the range of products and concentrated on making better use of resources and on more efficient production

As a result of his policy, annual sales have increased rapidly during the last five years, and the sales output per employee has almost doubled; Bellcrest is now a successful profit-making concern. Hanson also learned that Malone is looking out for opportunities to expand and diversify while Downes is very cautious about changing his policy.

At a meeting at the Bank, Sir Frederick Ashburnham expressed his satisfaction at Bellcrest's recovery, indicated by the rise in share prices and the increase in the final dividend. He told Downes that, in Edward Needham's view, Bellcrest no longer needed the loan, and the Bank might decide to withdraw it in order to reinvest the capital with an expanding competitor with development plans.

Downes was taken aback at this news and had to agree to let the Bank have detailed proposals of Bellcrest's development plans within the next two months in the hope of persuading the Bank to allow Bellcrest to keep the loan.

Downes' first course of action after this unexpected turn of events was to call at Malone's home the same evening. He instructed Malone to look at all Bellcrest's development projects and to report back to him with his recommendations.

EXERCISES

Exercise A **Complete the following sentences:**

1 An is a man who puts his money into a business. If he i. his money in a company, he usually buys in that company and is known as a . Instead of a fixed r. of i. he usually receives a d. on his capital.

2 Unless a company holds a monopoly, it has to with rival firms. The existence of is a factor no company can ignore; indeed, many companies keep a constant eye on the activities of their

3 Before a company decides to introduce a new product it must ensure that there is a for it. To find out whether it can the product, a company will often conduct a m. s. . Most companies have a M. M. who is in charge of sales promotion.

Exercise B **Make sentences from these notes:**

Examples:
Bellcrest/make/electronic components?
Does Bellcrest make electronic components?
Malone/want/diversify/product range.
Malone wants to diversify the product range.

1 Orpenshaw/work/research and development department.
2 Downes/carry/heavy responsibility.
3 Evans/not/Board of Directors.
4 Bellcrest/manufacture/electronic components?
5 Ashburnham/not/want/continue/loan/Bellcrest.
6 When/you/want/my report?
7 Downes/not/understand/Needham/arguments.
8 He/delay/every decision/until/too late.
9 You/have/plans/development?
10 We/not/know/why our products/not/sell.

Exercise C **Complete these sentences:**

1 Five years ago Smith & Co. only (manufacture) bicycles.

2 They always (sell) most of their products on the home market but (export) some of them to Africa.

3 In 1968 foreign competition (increase) and sales (drop) sharply.

4 The Board of Directors (feel) that the company (must) diversify.

5 They (plan) to get a loan from the Bank and as the company (enjoy) a high reputation, they (have) no difficulty in getting one.

6 They (spend) this money on development and (begin) production of motorcycles a few weeks ago.

7 Hanson (write) a very interesting article on Bellcrest.

8 Bellcrest (take over) a smaller company last year.

9 Their competitors (read) about it in the Financial Times.

10 One customer (buy up) our complete stock.

Exercise D **Make sentences from the table below:**

Example *a) Bellcrest's designs are reliable*

b) True. But on the other hand, Davidson's designs are more effective.

	designs		effective
Bellcrest's	marketing techniques		good
	products	is	successful
Our company's	production methods	are	efficient
	salesman		quick
Davidson's	service		slow
	delivery		bad

Exercise E **Written Task**

When Downes returns to Bellcrest after his meeting with Sir Frederick Ashburnham at the Bank, he has to write a letter confirming the points raised during the discussion. You write this letter for him. Use these notes:

Surprised at possible withdrawal of bank loan.
Agree to produce development plans within two months.
Trust no action will be taken until then.

DRILLS

Drill 1 The Bellcrest works are in London, I believe.
NO, ACTUALLY THEY AREN'T IN LONDON.

Oh, surely they make electrical machines.
NO, ACTUALLY THEY DON'T MAKE ELECTRICAL MACHINES.

Drill 2 I wonder what products Bellcrest manufactures.
YES, WHAT PRODUCTS DOES BELLCREST MANUFACTURE?

And I wonder why Williams resigned.
YES, WHY DID WILLIAMS RESIGN?

Dialogue *George Hanson arrives at Bellcrest.*

Hanson: Good morning, I have an appointment to see Mr. Malone, the Marketing Manager, at 11.15.

Hanson: Hanson. George Hanson.

Hanson: Thank you very much.

Hanson: Yes, that's right.

Hanson: How do you do? I hope I'm not putting you to any trouble.

Drill 3 **Notes:**

1 The works
2 Our sales company
3 Managing Director
4 Supplement
5 You
6 An explanation
7 Their contract
8 The Board

Drill 4 *Paul Malone is introducing his associates to visiting journalists.*

1 Managing Director/Downes
2 Sales Manager/Evans
3 Chairman/Downes
4 Company Secretary/Spence
5 Head of Research/Orpenshaw
6 Personnel Manager/Jenkins
7 Production Manager/Driver
8 Transport Manager/Mackenzie

ACTIVE LISTENING

George Hanson, a journalist, is questioning Malone about Bellcrest.

1 How much did Hanson know about the history of Bellcrest before he talked to Malone?

....

....

2 Why did Downes have to put the company back on its feet?

....

....

3 What was Bellcrest's reputation before Downes came?

....

....

4 Why didn't Bellcrest have enough money to continue their research five years before?

....

....

5 What action did the company then take?

....

....

6 Why was Edward Needham appointed to the Bellcrest Board?

....

....

7 How long did Downes wait before cutting out unprofitable lines?

....

....

8 What does Malone think about Bellcrest's present markets?

....

....

9 What details does Malone give Hanson about new fields he plans to go into?

....

....

10 What is Hanson's reaction to this?

....

....

ROLE SIMULATION

Statement of Problem

When Downes introduced his new policies designed to put Bellcrest back on its feet, it was not only Donald Williams who resigned. There were a number of resignations from men occupying key positions within the company.
The posts that fell vacant at that time were those of Personnel Manager, Transport Manager, Distributor Sales Manager, Supply Manager, Deputy Company Secretary and Deputy Head of Research and Development.

Bellcrest advertised these posts and received a great many applications. On the basis of the curriculum vitae submitted, a short list of three candidates was drawn up for each post, and those selected were asked to attend an interview. Downes formed a selection board to conduct the interviews consisting of himself, Paul Malone and Bob Orpenshaw.

The problem confronting the panel is therefore to select the most suitable applicant of the three applying for each post.

en follow-up

You are Downes. Write two letters to two of the candidates you have interviewed, one offering the candidate the job, the other rejecting the candidate.

DESCRIPTION OF ROLES

Maurice Downes
You are the Chairman of the selection board and are therefore responsible for leading each interview. You may allot particular areas of each interview to Malone or Orpenshaw. Remember you will have to decide which candidate to appoint.

Malone
You are the Marketing Manager and should approach each interview with your marketing requirements firmly in mind. You are free to invent your requirements.

Orpenshaw
You are the Head of Research and Development and should approach each interview with the needs of your department firmly in mind. You are free to invent your requirements.

Each member of a selection board
Before you interview a candidate, you should work out your attitude to the following points:—
The salary you will offer.
The qualifications you require for the job.
What value to put on the candidate's previous experience.
The prospects you can offer at Bellcrest.
You should think up some other points to raise with the candidate.

Each Candidate

Before being interviewed you should think out an imaginary curriculum vitae.
You should also work out your attitude towards such questions as:—

Salary.	Holidays
Prospects with Bellcrest	Reponsibilities

You should think up other points which you may wish to raise at the interview.

Supplementary Exercise

Complete the following sentences:

1 When you see an advertisement for a job, and you want to a. for the job, you send in an a.

2 You usually enclose a c. v. with your letter.

3 If there are a great many c. for a single job, a company usually draws up a s. l.

4 Candidates are then asked to come to an i. , which may be before a s. b. or with a single person.

5 The a. is made on the basis of the interview and r. from people who know the candidate.

Name

Date of Interview:

Time

Married/single age children

Health

Willingness to travel

Manner and Appearance

Education and Qualifications (summarize)

Present Position

Experience

Administrative ability

Social ability, relationships

Ability to work under stress

Initiative

Motivation (goals)

Leisure Activities and Interests

Present Salary

Date from which available

Expenses Paid/to be paid

THE SC1

It came as a complete surprise to Downes that the Bank was considering withdrawing the £300,000 loan it had advanced five years ago. To keep the loan Downes would have to supply the Bank with details of convincing development projects, before he was in a position to do so. Immediately after the meeting with the Bank, Downes called at Malone's home and told him to look into the question of suitable projects and report back to him as quickly as possible. Malone promised that there would be a report on his desk the following Monday.

The following morning Malone asked Evans and Orpenshaw to come to his office to review all the development projects Bellcrest had undertaken in the last five years and consider which project should be given priority. It very soon became clear that Evans wasn't in favour of any of the projects. Although the projects were good in themselves, he felt that from a sales point of view there was little chance of their giving Bellcrest the edge over their competitors. It was also true, as Evans went on to say, that some of the projects had been suspended and were also well outside Bellcrest's normal field of operations. To Orpenshaw, on the other hand, there was no question which project to support. It was obvious that the SC1 was the one to back. The SC1 was a speed control mechanism for vehicles driven by electricity, such as electric vans and fork-lift trucks. There are considerable advantages in using such a device, but it had been decided to suspend the SC1 five years ago, a decision that had led directly to the resignation of Donald Williams.

Malone realized that it would be extremely difficult to revive the SC1. Despite its technical advantages, there was no established market for it, and it had not been fully developed before its suspension. Malone worked on the SC1 files all weekend, having instructed Evans and Orpenshaw to meet him again the following Monday.

At the second meeting, Evans was still very much against the SC1, whereas Orpenshaw was whole-heartedly in favour of it. Five years ago the arguments against the SC1 were primarily that there were poor prospects for sales in the industrial vehicle sector and that it would have taken five years for Bellcrest to break even and longer to show a profit. It had not been clear at the time whether a market existed among car manufacturers and an added consideration was Bellcrest's lack of experience in the automotive field. There had also been the bad cost price ratio to take into account.

Malone was quick to realize that these arguments no longer held water. It was possible that with everyone wanting to get rid of pollution there already was a potential market for the SC1 in the private vehicle sector. Moreover, the prospects in the industrial vehicle sector had improved. Production costs could be cut, as Orpenshaw could easily design-in new components that would be cheaper and more efficient.

Eventually it was decided to submit the SC1 to Downes as a project deserving priority. Despite its being controversial, Malone was convinced he had taken everything into consideration and was in a position to support his choice of the SC1 with solid arguments.

Downes' immediate reaction on seeing Malone's report was to call in the Company Secretary, Charles Spence. Spence was immediately against the SC1 because of the expense involved in developing it, although he admitted it was a fine technical achievement. Despite Malone's offering to answer his questions, Spence remained highly sceptical of the SC1. Malone mentioned that his department had enough money for a market study. Downes refused to commit himself, and Malone was left to wait for his decision.

EXERCISES

Exercise A **Complete the following sentences:**

1 Downes, Spence and Malone met to d. the threatened withdrawal of the loan. A p. to revive the SC1 was put forward. A number of important points had to be t. into a. before a d. could be reached. Malone was in f. of the SC1 but Spence was very much a. it and raised several o. Spence and Malone had an a. over the advantages and d. of the SC1 and it was clear that the matter was going to need careful c. In the end, Downes a. to keep an open mind on the SC1.

2 Five years ago the SC1 was s. . Williams, who was in charge of the project, felt that it was being a. and left the company. Nobody was quite sure if he had r. or been d.

Exercise B *These are the notes Malone made while discussing the SC1 project with Orpenshaw and Evans. Later he had to write up these notes into a report.* **Write the sentences for him as in these examples:**

. . . . . lot of development work/still/do.
THERE WILL BE A LOT OF DEVELOPMENT WORK STILL TO DO.
. . . . . obvious/prospects/improve.
IT IS OBVIOUS THAT PROSPECTS WILL IMPROVE.

1 . . . . . sharp competition/other companies.
2 . . . . . likely to strain/production resources.
3 . . . . . a period/don't show a profit.
4 . . . . . many people/think/project/too ambitious.
5 . . . . . expanding market/automotive field.
6 . . . . . big increase/use of electric vehicles/next five years.
7 . . . . . true/must make/careful market study.
8 . . . . . possible/reduce production costs/designing-in cheaper components.
9 . . . . . good sales opportunities/variable speed control mechanism.
10 . . . . . enough money in the budget/market study.

Exercise C **Report this Dialogue. Choose the best verb from this list:**
decide/tell/want/offer/remind/advise/agree/promise/arrange/ask.

Example: *Jean, get Orpenshaw on the phone.*
Malone told Jean to get Orpenshaw on the phone.

Malone: Jean, get Orpenshaw on the phone.
Orpenshaw? Would you mind coming up to my office straight away? I want todiscuss development projects.

Orpenshaw: I'll bring all the files, shall I?

Malone: Yes. Oh, and don't forget to bring the results of the market study on the BX3.

Later in Malone's office.

Malone:	You'd better put all that in writing, Bob.
Orpenshaw:	O.K. I'll write a full report.
Malone:	I'd like you to give it to Evans by the end of the week.
Orpenshaw:	I'll definitely have it ready by Thursday.
Malone:	Well, we'll meet again on Friday morning. Could you be here at 10? Jean, put that in my diary.

Exercise D **Choose the most appropriate word from this list:**

suitable/ly	potential/ly	private/ly
technical/ly	doubtful/ly	immediate/ly
useful/ly	whole-hearted/ly	high/ly
efficient/ly	primary/ly	normal/ly

I know that the SC1 has Malone's ________ support, but I must say, Maurice I feel ________ about the whole project. Of course the design of the SC1 is ________ advanced, but Bellcrest has no ________ experience of selling to the ________ vehicle sector. This is a ________ competitive field and my big fear is that we may not be able to produce the goods as ________ as our rivals. It might be difficult for us to take advantage of the ________ market. I am ________ concerned with the cost of this project. Production costs for the SC1 would be ________ so we cannot expect an ________ profit. I think the BX3 project would be much more ________

Exercise E **Written Task**

Answer this letter:

The Morford Vehicles Co. Ltd.,
Lagos,
Nigeria.

17th October, 19 . . .

The Sales Manager,
Bellcrest Ltd.,
Leicester,
England.

Dear Sir,

We have seen your advertisement in 'The Motor Mechanic' and are interested in electronic components for the industrial vehicle sector.

Please send detailed specifications of the BX3, quoting your price C.I.F. Lagos and stating terms of payment, discounts for regular purchases and delivery dates.

As we have considerable requirements in this field, could you please also send us a catalogue.

Yours faithfully,

James White
(Chief Buyer)

DRILLS

Drill 1 *Paul Malone and Charles Spence are arguing about what happened five years ago when the SC1 was suspended.*

Look, we decided to abandon the SC1.
I'M SORRY, BUT IT WAS NEVER DECIDED TO ABANDON THE SC1.

We had a sound reason for suspending the SC1.
I'M SORRY, BUT THERE WAS NEVER A SOUND REASON FOR SUSPENDING THE SC1.

Drill 2 *Malone is answering questions put to him by an assistant.*

What sort of design is it?
IT SEEMS TO ME IT'S RATHER GOOD.

How fast does he work?
IT SEEMS TO ME HE WORKS RATHER QUICKLY.

1 Good/well
2 Quick/quickly

3 Keen/keenly
4 Bad/badly
5 Efficient/efficiently
6 Slow/slowly
7 Good/well
8 Enthusiastic/enthusiastically
9 Urgent/urgently
10 Uncertain/uncertainly

Dialogue Opening a meeting

Paul Malone is opening a meeting at which he will be chairman.

Good morning, gentlemen. Please sit down.
Are we all here?
Let's make a start then, shall we?
Now, you've all had a copy of the agenda, haven't you?
Right, let's get down to business.
Can we deal with that under Any Other Business?
Yes. Charles, would you care to comment on that?

Drill 3 *Paul Malone is discussing the SC1 with Evans and Orpenshaw.*

Evans: Well, it seems obvious that we've got to carry out a Market Survey.

Malone: AS I SEE IT, THE THING WE'VE GOT TO CONSIDER IS *WHEN* TO CARRY OUT A MARKET SURVEY.

1 When?	3 How?	5 When?	7 How?
2 Where?	4 How?	6 When?	8 When?

Drill 4 *a) Malone, Evans and Orpenshaw are still discussing the SC1. Unfortunately, Orpenshaw doesn't agree with the ideas of the other two.*

Evans: My feeling is that we should review *all* the projects before going into details.

Orpenshaw: WOULDN'T IT BE BETTER TO GO INTO DETAILS FIRST?

b) Orpenshaw is rather rude when he disagrees in that way with his colleagues. Listen to him now, when is he being more polite:

Evans: My feeling is that we should review *all* the projects before going into details.

Orpenshaw: FORGIVE ME, BUT WOULDN'T IT BE BETTER TO GO INTO DETAILS FIRST?

c) Sometimes you may want to use another phrase, instead of 'Forgive me, but . . .':

Evans: The best thing would be to select a project and then discuss it with Downes.

Orpenshaw YOU MAY HAVE A POINT THERE, BUT WOULDN'T IT BE BETTER TO DISCUSS IT WITH DOWNES FIRST?

ACTIVE LISTENING

Tom Driver is Bellcrest's Production Manager, He is discussing the news that the SC1 may be revived with Malone's assistant.

1 How did Driver find out about the SC1?

. . . .

. . . .

2 How did Malone's assistant find out about it?

. . . .

. . . .

3 Is the project secret or has the company told its employees about it?

. . . .

. . . .

4 How do they think this information became known?

. . . .

. . . .

5 What is Driver's general attitude to the possible revival of the SC1?

. . . .

. . . .

6 What does he think Downes' attitude will be?

. . . .

. . . .

7 Do the two men think there is a lot of support for the project?

. . . .

. . . .

8 What do they think about the market for the SC1?

. . . .

. . . .

9 What is Spence's reputation?

. . . .

. . . .

10 Does Driver agree with Spence's position on the SC1?

. . . .

. . . .

What do you understand by the following expressions:

1 We thought it was completely hush-hush at this stage.

. . . .

. . . .

2 This has really been his baby ever since then.

....

....

3 It might give us the edge over our competitors.

....

....

4 It's rather a step into the dark, isn't it?

....

....

5 You know what a tight-fisted old so-and-so he is.

....

....

6 With him it's like getting blood out of a stone.

....

....

ROLE SIMULATION

Statement of Problem

At one point during the course of discussions at Bellcrest as to whether to take up development of the SC1 again, Malone decided to call all interested parties together to a meeting. The purpose of the meeting was to come to a firm decision as to whether or not to develop the SC1. Those present at the meeting were Malone and his assistant, Spence and his assistant, Orpenshaw and his assistant, Evans, Driver and his assistant, and the Head of the Market Research department.

You should re-enact this meeting. The purpose of it is to come to your own decision, as if you were representing Bellcrest Ltd., as to whether to submit the SC1 to Downes as a development project deserving top priority or not.

The letters SC1 stand for AC Variable Speed Control, Mark 1. It is a speed control mechanism for vehicles driven by electricity, such as electric vans. Up till now these vehicles have worked off batteries, but the batteries are big and heavy, and can store only a limited amount of electrical power. They have to be recharged frequently. A fork-lift truck, for example, keeps stopping and starting. Every time it changes speed, it demands more power from its engine. Every time this demand changes, a lot of power – in the form of direct current from the battery – is lost. By changing the direct current into alternating current the SC1 would save a lot of power.

Written follow-up Write up the minutes of the meeting.

EPISODE 3 MEETINGS

Malone submitted his report to Downes, in which he strongly recommended that the SC1 should be given priority over other development projects. Downes did not commit himself, but called a management meeting to discuss the report.

Downes opened the meeting by summarizing the position Bellcrest was in. He mentioned that Ashburnham's Bank had suggested that Bellcrest should repay the £300,000 loan made five years previously, unless the company needed the money to finance new developments. This move by the Bank meant that Malone had had to finalize his proposals for product development somewhat earlier than Downes had originally intended. He went on to invite the comments of those present on Malone's report.

Driver, as Production Manager, pointed out that producing the SC1 would be far from easy. Several products were being run down, however, and by adapting existing machinery some spare production capacity could be gained in the factory. He suggested that if Bellcrest wanted to introduce a new product line, they should start planning for it at once, as it was a suitable time to do this.

Spence accepted Driver's point about launching a new product line at the most suitable time, but questioned whether the SC1 was the most suitable product. He pointed out that Malone was recommending that they should revive a project that had been suspended by the Board five years previously. The Board would be unlikely to view its return favourably. He also wondered whether Malone was recommending that they should abandon current projects, on which a great deal of money had been spent over the last two years, in favour of the SC1, and went on to raise further objections on the grounds of expense and the uncertainty of the market.

Despite Spence's constant objections, Malone was able to defend the SC1 and gain the support of the meeting for the project. Although at the end of the meeting Spence still had reservations, Malone succeeded in getting a general agreement that new product development should be centred on the SC1. After the meeting, Downes warned Malone in private that the blame for any failure of the SC1 project would rest on his shoulders. He also stressed the need for absolute security.

As soon as he had management support Malone started work on getting the SC1 project off the ground. In consultation with Evans he decided to call in a firm of management consultants, M.P. Consultants, to carry out a market survey. He also suggested that they should engage a product executive who would be solely responsible for marketing the SC1. He recommended that they should approach Alan Beeston, who had had dealings with Bellcrest when he worked for the Ministry of Defence and was now looking for a job.

The decision taken at the management meeting was an important one for Bellcrest. Equally important was a chance meeting in an aeroplane over the Atlantic between Donald Williams, formerly Marketing Manager of Bellcrest, and now Managing Director of Electrovans, and Sam Urwin, Executive Vice-President of Passlee Electronics, a Canadian corporation and one of Bellcrest's largest overseas customers.

Urwin was on his way to Bellcrest, and Williams suggested that he should also visit Electrovans to have a look at their vehicle components, as to the best of his knowledge Bellcrest was not involved in the automotive field. When, after his arrival in England, Urwin mentioned this invitation to Downes and Malone during a game of golf, he was surprised at their obvious concern.

EXERCISES

Exercise A **Complete the following sentences:**

1 Malone wanted to be quite sure that there was a p. ______ market for the SC1, so he decided to c. ______ a market s. ______. He called in a firm of m. ______ c. ______ who were s. ______ in marketing.

2 Some time ago Bellcrest invested a considerable amount in new buildings and machinery, so their p. ______ f. ______ are now first-class. However, a new p. ______ l. ______ like the SC1 would put a strain on their p. ______ r. ______. It was necessary to plan immediately so that the p. ______ c. ______ of their factory could be increased. Bellcrest still had many p. ______ l. ______ which had not yet reached the end of their l. ______ c. ______

3 The amount of money a company sells its products for is the *price* of the product.
A company *prices* its products carefully.
What a company pays for materials or labour is the *cost* of materials or the *cost* of labour.
When a company *costs* a product, it decides how much money it will need to develop, produce and market the product.
If the company gets back in sales as much as it spends, then it *covers its costs.*
If a project is too *expensive*, the company abandons it, because it means too much *expense.*
The total amount of money paid out each year by a company is the annual *expenditure.*
When a businessman pays money to travel for his company, he can claim travel *expenses.*

a Development of the BX10 was stopped because it was too ______
b We'll have to buy the BX13 from Bellcrest although it's ______ rather high.
c Spence opposed the SC1 on the grounds of ______
d Do you know the ______ of raw materials?
e Our ______ on marketing has increased over the last year.
f We had to make price increases because of the ______ of labour.
g We can't spend so much on development if we're going to ______ our ______
h The manufacturers won't buy these components if the ______ is too high.
i After taking a visitor from Electrovans out to lunch, Mr Malone claimed ______ from Bellcrest.
j We'll have to ______ the development of this product line very carefully.

Exercise B **Make sentences from these notes:**

Example: *Bellcrest/complete/in the electronics field.*
Bellcrest is used to competing in the electronics field.

1 Bellcrest's Sales Manager/work/for Davidson's before.

2 An experienced salesman/deal with/awkward questions.
3 Our Managing Director/be/against this project.
4 This mechanism/control/the speed of the vehicle.
5 M.P. Consultants/prepare/market surveys in the automotive field.
6 Sometimes a bank loan/finance/new production facilities.
7 Beverman and Jones/export/components to Germany ten years ago.
8 Fork-lift trucks/carry/the goods to the store.
9 Malone/submit/reports to Downes/by now.
10 Modern production lines/increase/production capacity.

Exercise C **Make sentences from the table below:**

Example: a) *Abandoning the research project is going to waste money.*
b) *Yes. Abandoning a research project always wastes money.*

introduce finance abandon suspend sell	the	new product line research project machinery development plan	is going to	be expensive increase profits save money be difficult waste money

Exercise D **Fill in the blanks using should/shouldn't/would/wouldn't:**

Malone: Right, Dennis, let's get down to business. Now what about this market study? Which of the management consultant firms ______ we go to?

Evans: Management consultants? Is that really necessary? ______ it be possible to do that ourselves?

Malone: Oh, no, Dennis. This job is far too big for us. It ______ be done by an outside firm. It ______ do to make any mistakes, ______ it?

Evans: Well, in that case I think M.P. Consultants ______ be the best people to go to. After all, they're specialists in marketing, so they ______ be able to answer all our questions.

Malone: How long ______ we give them to complete the study?

Evans: Well, that rather depends on how soon we want it. It ______ take them long. They're very efficient. They ______ manage to get it done by the end of the month. I think my assistant ______ go and see them in person. The chief consultant is a friend of his. If he explained the position, they ______ probably give it priority.

Exercise E **Written task**

Williams met Sam Urwin on the plane. In the hope that Passlee Electronics would eventually do business with Electrovans, Williams wrote a follow-up letter to Urwin.

Write this letter for him. Use these notes:

it was most pleasant
feel sure you will be interested
hope you will be able to visit
Tuesday 29th
offer him dinner

DRILLS

Drill 1 *Bellcrest's Personnel Manger is answering a recruit's questions about his new job.*

Do I have to write a report every day?
NO, YOU NEEDN'T WRITE A REPORT EVERY DAY.

What happens if I file documents in the wrong place?
YOU MUSTN'T FILE DOCUMENTS IN THE WRONG PLACE ON ANY ACCOUNT.

Drill 2 *Malone has met an old friend of his, and they are talking about Bellcrest's work.*

Do you make components for electric motors now?
NO, WE USED TO MAKE THEM.

Don't you find it difficult to work with transistors?
NO, WE'RE USED TO WORKING WITH THEM.

(You must choose which is the better answer – for example, 'We used to make them' or 'we're used to making them'.)

Dialogue **Closing a meeting**

After listening to everybody's opinions on the SC1 project, Downes closes the meeting.

I see. Now you've all had your say. Has anyone anything further they wish to raise?

Good. Are we all in favour of Malone's proposal?

What about you, Charles?

With reservations, but in favour. Minute that, please, Miss Armstrong.

The next meeting will be at the same time next week. Is that all right?

Now, is there any other business?

Good. In that case, I declare the meeting closed.

Drill 3 *Spence agreed to support the SC1, but with reservations. He is discussing his reservations with Paul Malone.*

Listen Charles. I'm sure the answer to our problems is diversification.
YES, THERE'S CERTAINLY A CASE FOR DIVERSIFICATION, ALTHOUGH IT'S A MAJOR CHANGE OF POLICY.

I still think we should revive the SC1.
YES, THERE'S CERTAINLY A CASE FOR REVIVING THE SC1, ALTHOUGH IT'S NOT IN OUR FIELD.

1 Major change of policy
2 Not in our field
3 Take time
4 Expensive
5 A waste of money
6 Cost a great deal
7 Too early yet
8 Difficult to persuade the Board

Drill 4 *Maurice Downes is Chairman of the Management Committee. One of a Chairman's important functions is to control the meeting, and keep to the correct order of business.*

Mr Chairman – I feel it's time we discussed costs.

BEFORE WE DISCUSS COSTS, MAY I DRAW YOUR ATTENTION TO PARAGRAPH 3 OF THE REPORT?

A good Chairman, when he guides a meeting in this way, lets the speaker know that he won't forget the point that was raised.

BEFORE WE DISCUSS COSTS, MAY I DRAW YOUR ATTENTION TO PARAGRAPH 3 OF THE REPORT? PERHAPS WE COULD RETURN TO THE QUESTION OF COSTS LATER?

1 paragraph 3 of the report
2 another point
3 the next point on the agenda

4 another important matter
5 the sales reports
6 this letter from the Bank
7 something we've overlooked
8 lunch arrangements.

ACTIVE LISTENING

Malone and his assistants have just returned from a meeting of the Management Committee and are discussing the SC1 project.

1 Why was it necessary to start planning immediately?

. . . .

. . . .

2 What will Orpenshaw's reaction to the decision be?

. . . .

. . . .

3 What is Orpenshaw planning to do?

. . . .

. . . .

4 Why does Malone think they should commission a market survey and what does he hope to get from it?

. . . .

. . . .

5 What disadvantage does his assistant point out?

. . . .

. . . .

6 How will the survey be financed?

. . . .

. . . .

7 Why might Dennis Evans be hurt if Malone approaches a firm of Management Consultants?

. . . .

. . . .

8 What does Malone propose to do so that Evans will not be hurt?

. . . .

. . . .

9 Which other problem do they discuss?

. . . .

. . . .

10 What does Malone want to do?

. . . .

. . . .

11 Why does he feel this is necessary?

. . . .

. . . .

12 Why does Malone think Alan Beeston is a suitable candidate for this post?

. . . .

. . . .

ROLE SIMULATION

Statement of Problem

After Malone had gained the support of Evans and Orpenshaw for the SC1, he still had to submit his proposal to Downes. Downes decided to call a meeting at management level to reach a formal decision as to whether to proceed with the SC1 or not. He invited Dennis Evans and Bob Orpenshaw to attend, in view of their involvement with the SC1.

The problem to be solved is whether to submit the SC1 to the Board of Directors as a priority for new product development. At management level there are further considerations to be taken into account, such as possible alternatives to the SC1, potential markets both at home and abroad, the Board's possible reaction to the proposal, the expense involved and the existence of competition. At this level, the SC1 project also raises matters of company policy, such as the question of whether Bellcrest should stick to its present field of operations or move outside this field to open up new ranges of products.

Written follow-up

Write a short report on the meeting, explaining the arguments for and against the SC1 and what decision was reached.

JOBS

Malone finds that getting the SC1 project under way is not going to be easy. The first setback occurs during his game of golf with Downes and Urwin. Urwin mentions that he is visiting Electrovans to have a look at their vehicle components. Now Malone has a problem. If he tells Urwin that Bellcrest is moving into the field of vehicle components, he will risk Electrovans getting to hear about the SC1. On the other hand if he doesn't tell Urwin that Bellcrest has plans to develop the SC1, Urwin will probably commit Passlee Electronics to buying from a competitor. Downes settles the matter by telling Malone not to reveal his plans yet.

A further complication arises the following day. Evans has seen Orpenshaw in the canteen and has just heard that Orpenshaw has been offered another job. Malone is extremely concerned about this, and immediately gets in touch with Orpenshaw, as he fully realizes that if Orpenshaw leaves Bellcrest there will be no chance of developing the SC1.

When Malone meets Orpenshaw he tries to find out who has approached him, but can get no more out of him than Evans did. Orpenshaw simply answers that he hasn't yet made up his mind about the job, and that he doesn't want to talk about it. He says he won't accept less money than he's getting at Bellcrest. Malone then reminds him of his importance to the SC1 project, but Orpenshaw merely points out it was his invention.

Unable to get a definite answer out of Orpenshaw, Malone takes the problem to Downes. Downes takes the news calmly and suggests that Malone should check up on the terms of Orpenshaw's contract of employment. He accepts the fact that if Orpenshaw leaves, that will be the end of the SC1 project. Malone suggests that it is Donald Williams who is trying to get Orpenshaw away from Bellcrest, but Downes thinks that it is more likely to be Urwin.

Malone has better luck when he interviews Alan Beeston. Beeston used to work for the Ministry of Defence and as he was then involved in negotiating contracts for electronic equipment for the army, he is used to dealing with the type of products that Bellcrest manufactures. Although he doesn't actually say so, Malone has Beeston in mind for the new post of Product Executive for the SC1. During the course of the interview it becomes more and more apparent that Beeston would be suitable for this post. He has had experience with electronic equipment while working for the Ministry, although he has only been involved in the buying side. At present he is working for Beamish Motors, and so has already gained some experience of the business world in general and the car industry in particular – an important point in Malone's eyes.

Later the same week Malone and Evans visit M.P. Consultants, the firm who are doing the market study for Bellcrest. Although the brief was clear, Dr Perkins wants to go over the terms of reference in more detail. Malone confirms that the three main areas in which Bellcrest are interested are industrial vehicles, commercial vehicles and small electric cars for use in cities. M.P. Consultants have just completed a survey on the use of cars in cities, and if Malone is interested, they will try to get permission for Bellcrest to have access to some of the data.

To Malone's surprise, he finds that M.P. Consultants have already been approached by another company interested in a market survey for a product similar to the SC1. In view of this unexpected news, Malone is even more anxious for a preliminary study of the market in the United Kingdom to be ready in four weeks' time. The existence of rivals to the SC1 is a possibility Malone had not anticipated.

EXERCISES

Exercise A **Complete the following sentences:**

1 Beeston left the Ministry of Defence because there seemed to be little p. of ever rising to a higher position. He had been there for five years and had not been p. . Beamish Motors had several v. to f. and they o. him a j. at a high salary, with good p. for p. . After he had signed the c. of e. he found out that he was stuck behind a desk all day doing boring routine paperwork. He wanted more j. s. so he asked the management if he could t. to one of their subsidiary companies.

2 Urwin came over from Canada to re-negotiate the l. a. between Passlee Electronics and Bellcrest. Under the t. of this a. Passlee is allowed to manufacture Bellcrest products in Canada. This does not, however, prevent them from n. c. with other companies.

3 Bellcrest commissioned M.P. Consultants to conduct a preliminary s. on the market prospects of the SC1. Their instructions were laid down in the b. that Malone sent to Dr Perkins. Their t. of r. included industrial vehicles, commercial vehicles, and electrically driven private vehicles. These were the three a. that interested Bellcrest and they asked the consultants to organize their report under these h. The company had already gathered some facts on the use of cars in cities and they offered to give Bellcrest the d. . As Bellcrest did not want anyone to know about their revived interest in the SC1, they asked the consultants to t. the matter as c.

Exercise B **Join the two phrases to make a sentence using 'if':**

Examples:
Orpenshaw resigning.
Williams offering him a job.

If Orpenshaw resigns, Williams will offer him a job.

The Bank withdrawing the loan.
Bellcrest not developing a new project.

The Bank will withdraw the loan if Bellcrest doesn't develop a new project.

1 Urwin visiting Electrovans.
Urwin enquiring about vehicle components.

2 Electrovans hearing about the SC1.
Malone informing Urwin.

3 Malone not informing Urwin.
Passlee Electronics buying from a competitor.

4 Electrovans competing with Bellcrest.
Bellcrest entering the private vehicle sector.

5 Bellcrest needing a product executive.
Bellcrest developing the SC1.

Example:
Orpenshaw deciding to stay.
Bellcrest offering him more money.

If Orpenshaw decides to stay, Bellcrest should offer him more money.

6 Bellcrest appointing Beeston.
The Board approving the new post.

7 Bellcrest treating the project as confidential.
Other companies competing.

8 Electrovans producing a speed control mechanism.
Bellcrest examining the patents carefully.

9 Bellcrest getting finance from other sources.
The Bank refusing to renew the loan.

10 The consultants confirming their fears.
Bellcrest accepting the facts.

Exercise C **Complete these sentences:**

1 Malone is worried because Urwin (visit) ______ Electrovans to have a look at their vehicle components. He (not want) ______ to tell Urwin that Bellcrest (move) ______ into the field of vehicle components. But if he (not tell) ______ Urwin about the SC1, he will risk Urwin buying from Electrovans. He also (think) ______ Williams (try) ______ to get Orpenshaw away from Bellcrest. Malone (take) ______ the problem to Downes who suggests it is Urwin who (try) ______ to take Orpenshaw from Bellcrest and if he (succeed) ______ there will be no chance of developing the SC1. Downes (settle) ______ the matter by telling Malone not to inform Urwin of Bellcrest's plans.

Exercise D **Complete the sentences from the notes:**

Examples:
M.P. Consultants/complete/survey/use/cars in cities/(just)

M.P. Consultants have just completed a survey on the use of cars in cities.

Beeston/have/any experience/electronics industry/(ever)?

Has Beeston ever had any experience in the electronics industry?

1 Other companies/show/interest/this market/(already).
2 The Ministry of Defence/draw up/terms/the contract/(yet)?
3 We/sell/components/private vehicle sector/before/(never).
4 Orpenshaw/not decide/accept the offer/new job/(yet).
5 You/think of/changing your job/(ever)?

6 Since 1965/Bellcrest/renew/the patents/(annually).
7 There/be/any consumer demand/electrically driven cars/(never).
8 Hanson/write/series of articles/the motor industry/(just).
9 The Directors/finished/discussing Malone's report/the SC1/(almost).
10 Malone/not tell/Urwin/Bellcrest's development plans/(yet)?

Exercise E **Written Task**

After Malone had interviewed Beeston, he prepared a memorandum for Maurice Downes.

Write this memo for him. Use these notes:

B.Sc. Manchester University.
Ministry of Defence for 6 years after graduation.
Contracts for electronic equipment.
With Beamish Motors for last year.
Interested in electronics industry – good ideas.

DRILLS

Drill 1 *Bellcrest employees are discussing the SC1.*

Evans tells me that Orpenshaw is about to leave.
WELL, IF ORPENSHAW LEAVES WE WON'T BE ABLE TO DEVELOP THE SC1.

But I heard he's going to stay.
WELL, IF HE STAYS WE SHOULD BE ABLE TO DEVELOP IT.

1 develop/SC1
2 develop
3 make/profit
4 make/profit
5 sell
6 sell
7 make/success
8 make/success
9 go ahead
10 go ahead

Drill 2 *Charles Spence has arrived in his office and has a number of questions to ask his assistant.*

When is Malone starting work on the SC1?
I THINK YOU'LL FIND DOWNES HASN'T APPROVED THE PROJECT YET.

When did Malone leave for London?
I THINK YOU'LL FIND HE'S ONLY JUST LEFT.

Notes
1 Downes/approve project – not yet.
2 He/leave – only just.
3 We/send off an invoice – only just.
4 They/complete the preliminary survey – nearly.
5 They/receive our letter – never.
6 Orpenshaw/send in an estimate – not yet.
7 They/deliver on time – always.
8 They/settle the account – already.

Dialogue **Transferring a telephone call**

Paul Malone is interviewing Alan Beeston when he is interrupted by a telephone call from Dr Perkins of M.P. Consultants.

Tell her I'll ring back later, would you?

Oh very well, put her through.

Malone here.

I see. Look, I'm afraid I'm rather tied up at the moment. Would you mind speaking to my Sales Manager?

Yes, I'm sure he'll be able to answer any questions you may have.

Yes, I'm looking forward to it as well. Hold on a moment, and I'll have you transferred.

Malone here. Would you transfer this call to Mr Evans, please?

Thank you very much.

Drill 3 *Malone and Spence are discussing the appointment of a product executive. Spence thinks Malone is not considering the question carefully enough, and raises objections to what he says.*

What I'm saying is we must have a product executive.
IT'S ALL VERY WELL FOR YOU TO SAY WE MUST HAVE A PRODUCT EXECUTIVE, BUT HAVE YOU CONSIDERED THE EXPENSE?

Oh, I think we just forget the expense, don't you?
IT'S ALL VERY WELL FOR YOU TO SAY WE JUST FORGET THE EXPENSE, BUT HAVE YOU CONSIDERED THE BOARD'S REACTION?

1 The expense
2 The Board's reaction
3 His qualifications
4 His actual experience
5 An actual figure
6 Dennis Evans' position
7 Beeston's actual duties
8 In any detail

Drill 4 *Dr Mary Perkins of M.P. Consultants rang Bellcrest the day before Evans and Malone went to her office in London. She spoke to Evans.*

a Hello, Dr Perkins. I hear you would like to discuss some points on the SC1 before we come to London tomorrow.
YES, I STILL DON'T UNDERSTAND *WHO* IS COMING TO LONDON TOMORROW.

b *Dr Perkins is being more polite.*
I hear you would like to discuss some points on the SC1 before we come to London tomorrow.
FORGIVE ME IF I'M BEING STUPID, BUT I STILL DON'T UNDERSTAND *WHO* IS COMING TO LONDON TOMORROW.

Notes

1 Who?
2 Why?
3 When?
4 Which?
5 What type?
6 What product?
7 When?
8 What time?

ACTIVE LISTENING

Mr Holmes, a marketing consultant, is being interviewed about the nature of his work.

1 What is the main function of a marketing consultant?

....

....

2 How does this help companies?

....

....

3 What work is involved in the launching of a new product or the redevelopment of an old one?

....

....

4 Why can't this be done by the regular staff?

....

....

5 Why is the marketing consultant only called in when a company steps outside its established field of activity?

....

....

6 Does the consultant usually get clear instructions from the company before beginning his investigations?

....

....

7 What must the consultant do first when he isn't given clear instructions.

....

....

8 What three things does the consultant consider when he defines the objectives of a company?

....

....

9 When is a questionnaire of little use?

....

....

10 When is a questionnaire relevant?

....

....

11 What problems are there as regards questionnaires?

....

....

12 What sort of people normally reply to these questionnaires?

....

....

13 How can one find out the opinions of the others?

....

....

14 What are the disadvantages of this?

....

....

ROLE SIMULATION

Statement of Problem

Up till now Bellcrest have kept the marketing, production and development departments separate from each other. Each department has had its own departmental head responsible directly to Maurice Downes as Managing Director. There have, of course, been frequent interdepartmental meetings at which the activities of each department have been co-ordinated in accordance with company policy, but there has been no overlapping of responsibility at lower levels between departments. The sales force, for example, have only been responsible for actually selling the products, and have not had to concern themselves in the least either with their development or with their production.

Now Malone has announced that he wants to appoint a product executive for the SC1, whose duty would be to plan for most of the activities affecting the profitability of the product, Such a post would naturally involve a degree of responsibility within the marketing, production and development departments, possibly within the finance department, at a lower than managerial level.

The Personnel Manager is fully aware that Malone's proposal to create the post of Product Executive for the SC1 is a controversial one. It involves a departure from standard company organization, and might well set a precedent leading to a complete reorganization of the structure of the company. Reluctant to approve Malone's proposal on his own initiative, he has called a meeting of those who would be affected by the creation of this post.

The object of the meeting therefore is to consider whether Malone's proposal is desirable in principle, to discuss what effect this would have on existing company structure and to work out the exact terms of reference the post of Product Executive would entail. The terms of reference would include, among other points, the areas of responsibility of the Product Executive within each department, to whom he would be directly responsible and for what, and what salary should be paid for such a post.

Existing Structure of Bellcrest

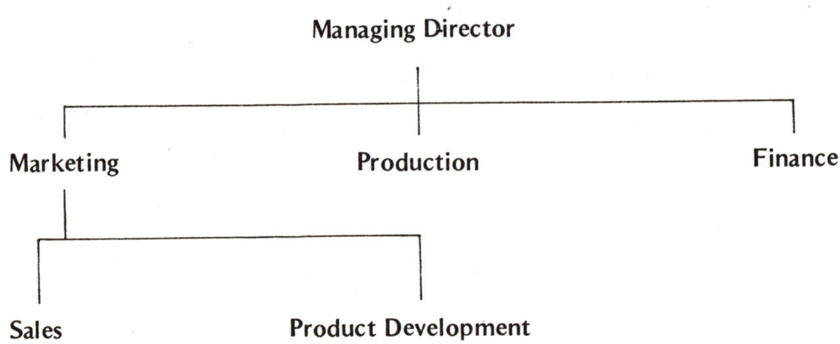

Written Task

Write a letter to a subsidiary company of Bellcrest Ltd., explaining to the Marketing Manager that a product executive for the SC1 is shortly to be appointed and defining his duties insofar as they will affect him.

AWKWARD QUESTIONS

Maurice Downes very much hoped to persuade Ashburnham's Bank not to withdraw the £300,000 loan given to Bellcrest five years before. He did not know who were Bellcrest's rivals for the Bank's money, and so decided to try to arrange a meeting with Sir Frederick Ashburnham to find this out. When his secretary rang up the Bank, Sir Frederick was speaking to someone else and the line was engaged. Downes had to wait until Sir Frederick rang him back.

When Sir Frederick rang Downes back, he enquired if Bellcrest had definite proposals for the Bank to consider. Downes said he would prefer not to go into details, and asked if Sir Frederick could spare twenty minutes to discuss Bellcrest's future. Unfortunately, Sir Frederick was shortly going to Brussels and was then flying on to Switzerland and the United States. Downes was disappointed at being unable to arrange a meeting with Sir Frederick, and was even more disappointed when Sir Frederick suggested he should discuss Bellcrest's future with Edward Needham, who was visiting another of the Bank's customers in Bellcrest's area. Sir Frederick did not tell Downes that the main purpose of Needham's trip to the Midlands was to visit Electrovans.

Downes met Needham for lunch later that day in a second-rate hotel, as Downes had been unable to book his guest into a more suitable one. The meal was very uninteresting, and there was a poor selection of wine. Downes had a tough steak and the meal was made more unpleasant for him by Needham's refusal to drink anything but water.

Downes was also unable to get the information about Bellcrest's rivals for the Bank's money. Throughout the meal Needham was clearly trying not to give anything away, and Downes had to be content with the knowledge that the Bank was comparing Bellcrest's growth rate with that of other companies who were trying to expand and diversify. But Needham failed to draw out Downes on the subject of Bellcrest's plans for diversification.

While Downes was trying to get more information from the Bank, Malone was attempting to get in touch with Urwin before he returned to Canada. Urwin finally rang him up from a petrol station, and agreed to have lunch with him on the following day, Saturday. Malone was slightly worried about entertaining Urwin at home as he had a number of awkward questions to ask him.

The question uppermost in Malone's mind at the time was whether it was Urwin who had offered Orpenshaw a job. This was particularly important to Malone in view of the SC1 to project, but he was unable to get Urwin to talk business until he was just about to leave. When he did manage to bring up the subject, he was surprised to hear that Urwin had offered a job not to Orpenshaw, but to his secretary, who had turned the job down. Urwin added that Malone was not paying enough attention to his secretary.

Just as Urwin was leaving Malone had a telephone call from Bellcrest's security officer, who told him there was a serious fire at the factory.

EXERCISES

Exercise A **Complete the following sentences:**

1 When people go out they often go to a r.   . If they're taking a guest they often b.   a t.   in advance as in popular restaurants it is sometimes difficult to get a table without a r.   . On arrival a w.   leads them to a table and brings them a m.   . Many restaurants have a w.   w.   , who brings them the w.   l.   to show them what there is to drink. It is usual to order the first two c.   together, and further c.   later in the meal. At the end of the meal a b.   will be brought.

2 A car runs on p.   . If you're in England you get p.   at a p.   s.   , known in America as a g.   s.   The a.   is the man who serves you. He will usually clean the w.   and b.   w.   for you while you are waiting. If you ask him, he will also t.   u.   the r.   with water, the b.   with distilled water, check that your t.   are at the right pressure and that you have sufficient o.

Exercise B **Make sentences from these notes:**

Example:
Bellcrest/run/loss/even after/Downes/takes over.
Bellcrest was running at a loss even after Downes took over.

1 Downes/stop/the SC1 project/when/take over/five years ago.
2 Orpenshaw/work/SC1 project/when/Downes/stop it.
3 Urwin/just/leave/when/Malone/receive/telephone call.
4 Dr Perkins/phone/Malone/while/interview/Beeston.
5 Malone/entertain/Urwin/when/hear/news of fire.
6 Malone/phone/Downes/when/hear/news of fire.
7 When/Downes/ring/Ashburnham/he/find/they/still/consider/withdraw/loan.
8 Hanson/visit/Bellcrest/because/write/series of articles.
9 Malone/dictate/letters/when/Evans/drop in.
10 Urwin/ring/Malone/while/wait/petrol station.

Exercise C *Downes and Malone are discussing the coming visit of the Minister of Science and Technology to the Bellcrest works.*

Complete the sentences with the most appropriate form of the verb, i.e. will do/is going to do/is doing:

Downes: Have you seen this letter from the Ministry?
Malone: Yes. I see they've confirmed the arrangements for the visit.
Downes: Yes. The Minister (come)   here next Tuesday. He (arrive)   on the 10.30 train.
Malone: Have you any plans for his visit? What (do)   he when he gets here?
Downes: Well, we have made one or two plans. We (show)   him round the new factory first.
Malone: Right. I (see)   that all that stuff left by the builders is cleared up.

Downes: Yes, please do. Oh, and make sure that those electric wires are properly fixed.

Malone: Heavens, yes! I had forgotten about that. Don't worry. I (have) a word with the chief electrician immediately.

Downes: He (talk) to some of the workers on the production line. It's a bit difficult to say how long this (take) possibly about an hour and half. Then we (have) lunch with members of the Board at 12.30. By the way, I haven't done anything about flowers for the table.

Malone: Oh, I have already talked to Jean about that, and she (look after) that.

Downes: Good. Then at two o'clock we (meet) to discuss Government plans to promote exports. They say they (help) companies that want to expand their export markets. If we can convince them that our development projects are sound, they (support) us financially.

Malone: Look. Orpenshaw says he (conduct) tests on the SC1 prototype next week. I'd like the Minister to see that.

Downes: Oh, yes. I promise you we (show) him that.

Malone: When is he due to leave?

Downes: He (travel) to London on the 4.30 train.

Exercise D **Complete the following sentences:**

1 Malone: Doesn't Sam Urwin know about the SC1?
Downes: No, and I (prefer) for the moment.

2 Driver: Are you going to try and persuade Orpenshaw to stay?
Malone: Yes, I (like) at Bellcrest.

3 Malone: Can you finish the report by the end of the week?
Orpenshaw: No, I (expect) until next week.

4 Spence: Can't we give the Bank details of our development project?
Downes: No, I (want) yet.

5 Spence: Why don't you consult Needham? After all, he's on the Board.
Downes: No, I (prefer) about this matter.

6 Orpenshaw: Will you be able to see Urwin before he leaves?
Malone: I'm not sure but I (hope) before he leaves.

7 Malone: What about Williams? He might cause trouble.
Downes: No, I (expect) to cause any trouble.

8 Spence: You'll have to be careful in your dealings with Ashburnham's.
Downes: Yes. I (not like) to withdraw the loan.

9 Downes: Will you get the results of the market survey soon?
Malone: I'm afraid not. I (expect) until the end of the month.

10 Secretary: Do you want to speak to journalists about the fire?
Malone: No, I (prefer) till tomorrow.

Exercise E **Written Task**

Write two letters in answer to this invitation as if you were Maurice Downes, one accepting it and one refusing it.

> The Chairman & Board of Directors request the pleasure of your company at a reception to be held to mark the 150th anniversary of the founding of Ashburnham's Merchant Bank on Wednesday, 3rd April, 1972 at 7 p.m.
>
> R.S.V.P. The Secretary to the Board
> Ashburnham's Bank,
> 96 Iberia Street,
> London WC29 SH5.
>
> White Tie
> Decorations will be worn.

DRILLS

Drill 1 I wonder if my assistant has written the report yet. Could you speak to him?
OH, DON'T WORRY ABOUT THAT. HE WAS WRITING THE REPORT WHEN I SPOKE TO HIM YESTERDAY.

I wonder if the Bank has arranged the loan. Could you ring them up?
OH, DON'T WORRY ABOUT THAT. THEY WERE ARRANGING THE LOAN WHEN I RANG THEM UP YESTERDAY.

Drill 2

a The telephone's ringing but I can't answer it.
DON'T WORRY. I'LL ANSWER IT FOR YOU.

b You could see Ashburnham next week if he wasn't going to Zurich.
OH, OF COURSE, I FORGOT. HE'S GOING TO ZURICH NEXT WEEK.

c Does Jean Smith intend to stay with Bellcrest?
OH, SHE'S CERTAINLY GOING TO STAY WITH BELLCREST.

Dialogue **At the petrol station**

On his way to visit Electrovans, Urwin stops to get some petrol:

Good morning. Six gallons, please.
Super, please. How much is super per gallon, by the way?
The battery's all right, but could you check the oil?
Well, you'd better give me a pint then, please.
Yes, I had the tyres checked only yesterday. Have you got a public telephone here?
Yes, fine. Oh, and would you clean the windscreen while you're at it?

Drill 3 *You are the host for dinner at a restaurant. The waiter has brought the menu, and you must offer various dishes to your guests.*

Waiter: Would you like any soup, sir?
NOW WHAT WOULD YOU LIKE? THERE'S ASPARAGUS, OR TOMATO OR PERHAPS YOU'D PREFER FRENCH ONION.

SOUP
Asparagus, tomato, French onion

FISH
Haddock, turbot, sole

MAIN COURSE
Roast beef, lamb chops, omelette

VEGETABLES
Spinach, broccoli, peas
Potatoes: boiled, roast, French fried

SWEETS
Fruit salad, trifle, ice-cream

COFFEE
English, Irish, Turkish

WINES
Claret, burgundy, hock

LIQUEURS
Cointreau, Crême de Menthe, Brandy.

Drill 4 *You are the guest at dinner. Unfortunately, you don't eat fish, and you don't drink beer.*

Now what would you like? The sole is very good here.
WELL, IF YOU DON'T MIND, I'D PREFER NOT TO HAVE FISH.

Well, what about an omelette?
THAT SOUNDS VERY NICE. YES, I'LL HAVE AN OMELETTE, PLEASE.

ACTIVE LISTENING

Paul Malone has invited Sam Urwin to lunch. He and Janet are planning the meal.

1 Where does their conversation take place?

. . . .

. . . .

2 Why didn't Paul tell Janet earlier?

. . . .

. . . .

3 Why is Saturday a bad day for Janet?

. . . .

. . . .

4 What is her attitude to Urwin?

. . . .

5 What is the main thing they must decide?

....

....

6 Why doesn't Janet want to have steak?

....

....

7 What does she choose for the first course and why?

....

....

8 Why do they decide not to have a sweet?

....

....

9 Have they already got the wine?

....

....

10 Why does Paul suggest going out the following Wednesday, and where will they go?

....

....

ROLE SIMULATION

Statement of Problem

Maurice Downes has three guests for dinner, Paul Malone and Dennis Evans each have two. None of the guests are English native speakers. For the sake of convenience, they have decided to entertain their seven guests together, and have booked a table for ten at the Crouch End Hotel, Leicester.

After a pleasant drink in the bar, they have led their guests into the dining-room and the waiter has presented the menu and the wine list.

The hosts now have to order the various courses for their guests, and explain the menu where necessary. They then have to entertain the guests for half an hour.

Written follow-up

Downes, Malone and Evans should write a letter to one of their guests thanking them for their visit.

The guests should write a letter thanking their hosts for their hospitality.

THE FIRE

As soon as Malone heard about the fire, he telephoned Downes, who was having lunch with Needham at the time. Malone, Downes and Needham all hurried immediately to the factory. The fire had started in an old warehouse, which had already been destroyed. Now the fire brigade were trying to prevent the fire from spreading. To do this they had to soak the research and development area, and the water was going to cause a lot of damage.

Needham was particularly concerned about whether the buildings had been insured, but Downes was able to reassure him on this point. The warehouse building was insured for £50,000 and the policy also covered the finished goods held in stock in the warehouse. He reminded Needham that it had been he who had questioned the premium Bellcrest paid, and so he should have known this.

They were interrupted by a journalist, Joy Banks. Downes admitted that if the fire spread it would be a disaster for Bellcrest. Joy Banks used his words out of context, and on Monday morning the Midland News headline quoted Downes as saying that the fire had been a disaster for the company.

This unfortunate publicity was bound to have a bad effect on Bellcrest shares, as Needham was quick to point out the following day. He offered to get the Bank's Public Relations agents to handle the press, radio and television, and Downes gratefully accepted.

The fire brought problems to everyone at Bellcrest. Most of Bellcrest's finished goods had been destroyed, quite apart from the damage done to the research and development area. Tom Driver, the Production Manager, had to deal with the most urgent problems. Production would have to be increased to make up for the losses, and he had to find additional storage space for new stocks. He also had to meet the insurance adjuster.

Spence, the Company Secretary, was concerned about the financial position of the company. Bellcrest had lost £200,000 worth of stocks, and he had to put in a claim to the insurance company as soon as possible. Evans naturally had dozens of telephone calls from customers worried about delays to their deliveries. Orpenshaw's research and development area had been soaked to prevent the fire from spreading. Water was nearly as bad as fire, and there had been a lot of damage. This meant that work on the SC1 might be held up.

While he was tidying up the mess, Needham came in and in his disappointment Orpenshaw unintentionally revealed the existence of a new development project, although he didn't mention the SC1 by name. This had been something Downes had particularly wanted to avoid, as he hadn't wanted the Bank to know anything about the SC1 until the Board had approved the project.

At twelve o'clock Downes held a management meeting to discuss the problems created by the fire. He invited Needham to attend. Driver was the first to describe his problems in detail. Additional storage space had to be found for finished goods, but if he re-allocated parts of the factory for storage purposes, production would be bound to suffer. Downes concluded that they might be obliged to look outside Bellcrest for the extra storage space they needed. Driver added that the factory would have to work to capacity for several weeks, and that overtime would almost certainly be needed as well.

Spence then went into the financial consequences of the fire. He said that Bellcrest were bound to have a short-term liquidity problem, and gave four reasons for this: the insurance claim would not be met for some time, Bellcrest would not be able to invoice customers for several weeks and at the same time would have to meet extra wage bills and the cost of renting new storage space.

At this point Needham was called away by an urgent phone call, and Malone immediately brought up the subject of the effect of the fire on the development of the SC1. Downes, however, refused to discuss it. He pointed out that the immediate need was to satisfy Bellcrest's customers. Malone replied that the obvious solution was to concentrate on the product lines that brought in the quickest returns and the largest profits, but went on to add that he did not think this was the course Bellcrest should follow. He recommended that Bellcrest should look after regular customers as far as possible, but pay special attention to overseas customers, who would be likely to bring in Bellcrest's long-term profits. The loss of overseas customers at this time would have a serious effect on the company's long-term growth. Evans had arranged to visit the more important U.K. customers, and it was agreed that Malone should visit customers and agents in Europe.

As the meeting broke up, Downes pointed out to Malone that unless the immediate problems were solved there would be no development of the SC1.

EXERCISES

Exercise A **Complete the following sentences:**

1 Needham was very concerned about whether the warehouse destroyed in the fire had been i. . Downes told him that the building had been i. f. £50,000, and that the p. also c. the stocks in the building. He told Needham that Bellcrest paid the i. c. a high p. . The following day the i. a. came to discuss Bellcrest's c. for the damage caused by the fire.

2 Spence told the meeting that Bellcrest would be short of cash for several weeks. He gave a number of reasons for this s. t. l. problem. Firstly, Bellcrest would not get c. from the insurance company immediately, as it would take time for the i. u. to meet the claim. Secondly, the company would not be able to i. customers, as there would be no goods being delivered. At the same time, he had to secure a short-term c. f. to meet extra wage bills for overtime.

Exercise B 1 *It is the Monday morning after the fire at Bellcrest.*

Make sentences from these notes, saying what people had to do at the time of the fire, and will have to do as a result of the fire.

Examples:
Security Officer/telephone/fire brigade.
The Security Officer had to telephone the fire brigade.

Needham/meet/Public Relations agents/this afternoon.
Needham will have to meet the Public Relations agents this afternoon.

a Fire brigade/prevent/fire/spread.
b Driver/find/additional storage space.
c Firemen/soak/R and D area.
d Malone/phone/Downes/immediately.
e Spence/put in/claim/insurance company.
f Miss Banks/interview/Downes.
g Malone/visit/customers in Europe.
h Press/take/photographs of the fire.
i Orpenshaw/tidy up/mess/soon as/can.
j Downes/stay up/most of the night.

2 *Downes and Needham are discussing what is bound to happen after the fire, and what they are obliged to do about it.*

Complete the sentences using 'bound to/obliged to'.

Downes: I'm afraid the damage is very serious. Production be affected and we be very short of storage space.

Needham: Do you mean you'll find storage space outside the factory?

Downes: Yes, I think we'll have to. And all the staff will   work overtime until we're on our feet again. Also the fire   delay the research work considerably.

Needham: Yes, I was just talking to Orpenshaw who has   tidy up the mess over there.

Exercise C *Mr Barker of Beamish Motors is writing to Malone about Alan Beeston.*

Complete the letter, choosing the appropriate verb form:

BEAMISH MOTORS LTD

23 Elder Road,
Birmingham 13.

PRIVATE AND CONFIDENTIAL
Our ref: PB/0095

Telephone: 021-839 2532

12th July, 1971.

P. Malone, Esq.,
Bellcrest Ltd.,
Leicester.

Dear Mr. Malone,

Alan Beeston

Thank you for your letter of 8th July, 1971.

Mr. Beeston (come)   to us last October on a year's contract. During his time here he (show)   considerable ability in his work and (be)   a useful member of our team. He (take)   a degree in electronic engineering at Manchester University eight years ago and (join)   the Ministry of Defence when he (leave)   university. His experience in negotiating contracts for the Ministry (be)   very valuable in his work here.

I (know)   Mr Beeston for five years and my experience of him leads me to believe that the work he (do)   at the Ministry after leaving University and the excellent work he (already do)   for us make him first class material for a post such as technical salesman or product executive.

Yours sincerely,

Peter Barker
Personnel Manager.

Exercise D *Example:*

a *Can I see you at 10 on Monday, the 6th?*

b *I'm afraid not. I'll be talking to journalists at 10, but I'll be free in the afternoon.*

DIARY

Monday
6th Talk to journalists 10 a.m.

Tuesday
7th Revise delivery dates with Evans 2.45

Wednesday
8th Speak to sales force 9.15

Thursday
9th Call on M.P. Consultants 10.30 a.m.

Friday
10th Discuss new designs with Orpenshaw 9.15

DIARY

Monday
13th Review the development projects with Downes 10.15

Tuesday
14th Meet Davidson's agent 9.45

Wednesday
15th Show visitors round new plant 2.30

Thursday
16th Attend Committee 11.00
Lunch with Spence 1.00

Friday
17th Interview candidates for post of Assistant Site Engineer 3.00

Exercise E **Written Task**

You are the chief buyer for a firm that deals with Bellcrest. You have learnt about the fire at their factory. Write a letter to Bellcrest. Use these notes.

just seen headlines
placed an order for . . . . early last month
require urgently . . . . not yet arrived
unfortunately if Bellcrest cannot supply . . . .

DRILLS

Drill 1 *The management at Bellcrest are discussing what to do after the fire.*

Should we ask the Bank for more money?
NO, I DON'T THINK SO. BUT I DO THINK WE SHOULD ASK FOR MORE TIME TO REPAY THE LOAN.

Are we obliged to meet existing delivery dates?
NO, I DON'T THINK SO. BUT I DO THINK WE'RE OBLIGED TO EXPLAIN THE POSITION TO OUR CUSTOMERS.

1 Ask/more time/repay/loan
2 Explain/position/our customers
3 Make/statement
4 Look/security arrangements
5 Work out/cost/damage
6 Remember/importance/long-term profits
7 Consider/short-term liquidity problem
8 Review/all our projects
9 Consider priorities/this area
10 Find/extra storage space/finished goods

Drill 2 We'll be in trouble if they withdraw the loan.
FORTUNATELY FOR US THEY HAVEN'T WITHDRAWN THE LOAN YET.

Of course we won't be able to invoice our customers for some time.
FORTUNATELY FOR US WE INVOICED OUR CUSTOMERS LAST WEDNESDAY.

1 Not yet
2 Last Wednesday
3 Last week
4 A few days ago
5 Just
6 Always – so far
7 Already
8 Last December
9 Never before
10 Yesterday

Dialogue **Talking to the Press**

Maurice Downes is interrupted by the journalist, Joy Banks, who has a number of questions to ask him.

Yes?
I can't give you a definite answer at the moment.
Yes, our insurance naturally covers everything.
Compensation?
Excuse me, I've forgotten your name.
Well, Miss Banks, I don't think this is the time to be talking about compensation. Now, if you'll excuse me, we're all very busy.
A press statement will be issued tomorrow morning. I have no further comment at this stage, Miss Banks.

Drill 3 *The Management Committee is meeting to discuss action after the fire. Downes, the Chairman, wants to make clear the priorities in the discussion.*

Don't you think it would be a good idea to talk to the Press?
OUR MAIN CONCERN NOW IS RESTARTING PRODUCTION, NOT TALKING TO THE PRESS.

1 Restart production
2 Find storage space
3 Build up stocks
4 Reassure customers
5 Service urgent orders
6 Solve the immediate problems
7 Bring in some money
8 Get quick returns

Drill 4 *Now the Committee is taking quick decisions. Downes does not ask for a formal vote, but simply asks if everyone is agreed.*

I feel we should make a statement to the Press.
CAN I TAKE IT WE'RE AGREED ON MAKING A STATEMENT TO THE PRESS?

Now Downes goes a step further, and suggests the action which is required.

I feel we should make a statement to the Press.
CAN I TAKE IT WE'RE AGREED ON MAKING A STATEMENT TO THE PRESS, IN WHICH CASE I'LL PREPARE A DRAFT.

1 Prepare draft
2 Tom Driver/make arrangements
3 Personnel Manager/issue notice
4 Paul/discuss it with Dennis Evans
5 Charles Spence/prepare statement
6 Paul/give instructions/Orpenshaw
7 Tom Driver/put up proposal
8 Miss Armstrong/circulate agenda

ACTIVE LISTENING

Mr Barrington, the insurance adjuster, visits Bellcrest after the fire. He is questioning Tom Driver about the fire.

1 Why wasn't the fire discovered immediately?

. . . .

. . . .

2 What had happened by the time the fire was discovered?

. . . .

. . . .

3 What action did the watchman take?

. . . .

. . . .

4 How badly damaged was the warehouse?

. . . .

. . . .

5 What was kept there?

. . . .

. . . .

6 What other damage had been done and what had caused it?

. . . .

. . . .

7 Does Driver know the value of this?

. . . .

. . . .

8 What new safety measures were Bellcrest considering at the time?

. . . .

. . . .

9 Who has all the information about Bellcrest's insurance policy?

. . . .

. . . .

10 Was the warehouse old-fashioned?

. . . .

. . . .

11 What is Bellcrest's system for keeping records?

. . . .

. . . .

12 Why were the stock records not lost in the fire?

. . . .

. . . .

ROLE SIMULATION

Statement of Problem

Maurice Downes has called a management meeting to hear reports from managers and heads of departments on the damage caused by the fire and to discuss what action should be taken to minimize its effects on the fortunes of Bellcrest.

You should re-enact this meeting and come to your own decision as to what action should be taken. Those present at the meeting will be Maurice Downes, in the chair, Paul Malone, Dennis Evans, Edward Needham, Tom Driver, Bob Orpenshaw, Charles Spence, David Smithson (Personnel Manager), Douglas Hamilton (Downes' assistant) and Miss Armstrong (Downes' secretary).

Ground plan of Bellcrest Ltd.

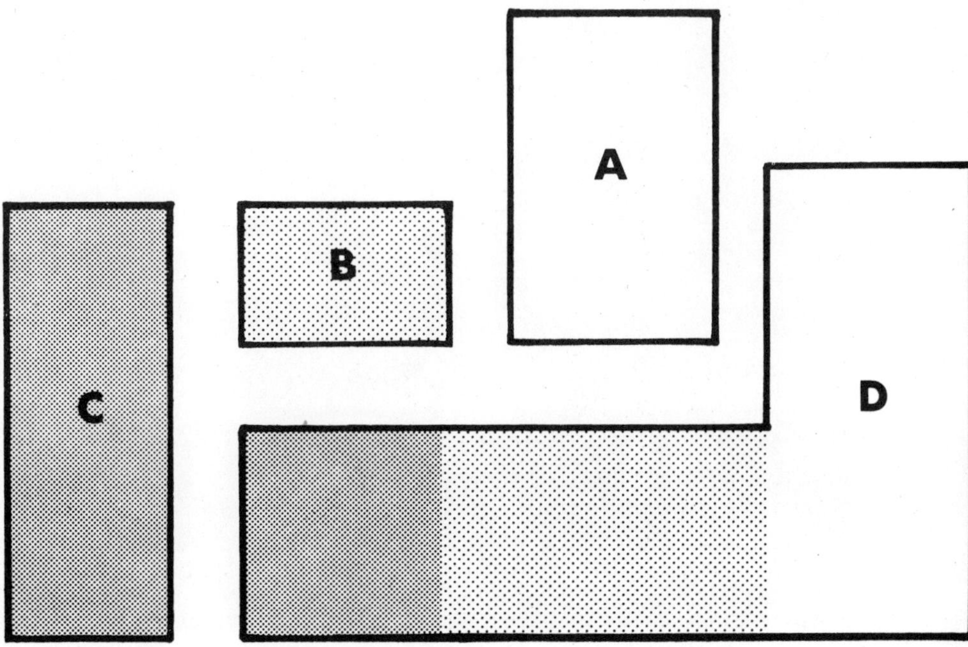

A Headquarters (Administrative/Personnel/Sales/Finance Departments)
B Research and Development Area
C Warehouse
D Factory

Destroyed by the fire.

Soaked in water by the fire brigade.

Written follow-up Write a report to a subsidiary company in Europe describing the effect of the fire and what action Bellcrest is going to take as decided at your meeting.

THE MARKET PLACE

Malone had to break off his work on the SC1 as it was necessary for him to visit important customers on the continent. He gave Jean his instructions as to his travel arrangements and went on to mention that Urwin had told him about his offering her a job. Jean replied that she had turned the job down, but on Malone's asking her why she had rejected the offer, she merely said that she had her reasons.

At this point Dennis Evans interrupted them. In view of inevitable delayed delivery dates, it was essential to get in touch with all Bellcrest's customers. Malone and Evans agreed that the sales force should approach customers individually and follow this up with something in writing. Malone emphasized that customers should be reassured that Bellcrest could still deliver the goods, and added that Evans himself should visit as many customers as possible after sending out an explanatory letter. Evans was not happy about writing this letter. as he felt he was better at talking than at writing, but Malone refused to write it for him, although he pointed out that it should go out over the Managing Director's signature. Evans found this letter extremely difficult to write.

Later that week, Evans and one of his salesmen, Finch, set out to visit Western Telecommunications. Finch was confident that Dobson, Western Telecommunications' chief buyer, would be easy to handle, but when Evans saw that Dobson was expecting a large order of surge diverters by the end of the month, he wasn't so sure. On meeting Dobson, Evans didn't waste time making excuses or explaining Bellcrest's problems, but came straight to the point and asked whether Western Telecommunications had sufficient stocks to enable Bellcrest to re-schedule its deliveries. By checking the stock levels, Finch established that Western Telecommunications had enough surge diverters to last for several months and that it would therefore be possible to re-schedule deliveries without disrupting Western Telecommunications' production.

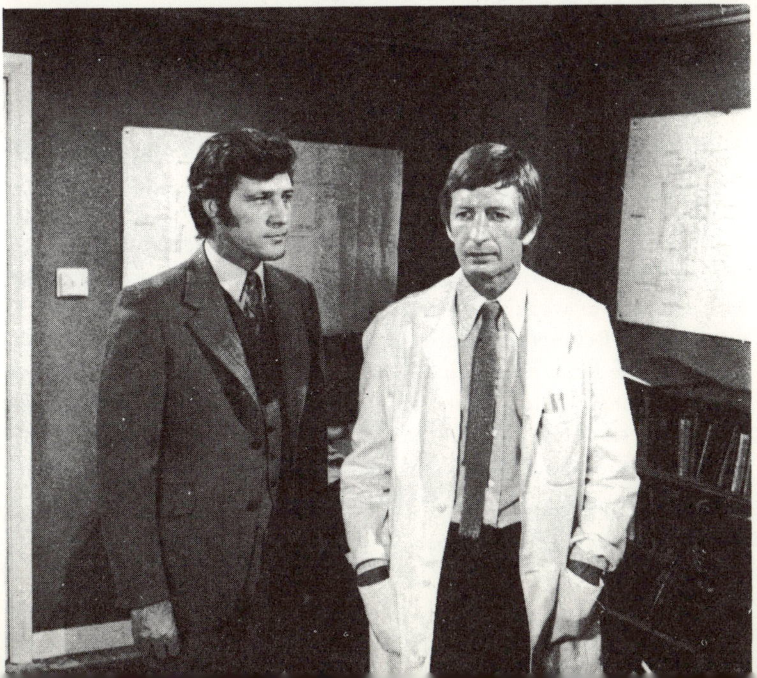

In spite of this, Dobson indicated that he was concerned about being over-dependent on Bellcrest for supplies, and pointed out that he would have found it almost impossible to find alternative supplies at short notice if the fire at Bellcrest had been bad enough to halt production for several months. He said that he had had several attractive offers from some of Bellcrest's competitors, although he hoped it wouldn't be necessary to turn to any of them. On signing the visitors' book on their way out. Evans found that a representative of an Electrovans subsidiary had already called on Western Telecommunications.

While Evans continued his tour of customers, Malone was preparing to set off for the Continent. Before he left, Bob Orpenshaw told him there was something he ought to know. He told Malone that he had decided to turn down the job he had been offered and went on to add that it was Donald Williams who had approached him. This didn't surprise Malone. Orpenshaw then revealed that Electrovans was working on an AC speed control device similar to the one patented by Bellcrest, and drew the conclusion that, as Electrovans' prototype infringed the Bellcrest patents, Williams wanted him to alter the design just enough to enable Electrovans to take out its own patent. Malone was naturally angry, and said that he would make sure that Williams learned about patents and their protection by law.

On arriving at the air terminal, Malone unexpectedly ran into Donald Williams returning from abroad.

EXERCISES

Exercise A **Complete the following sentences:**

1 Most companies employ a number of ______ to sell their products. Collectively they are known as the ______ and they come under the direction of the ______ Occasionally it is necessary for a company to launch a ______, also known as a ______, in order to promote sales of a particular product. In such a campaign the salesmen look for new ______ for the product, which means finding new customers.

2 Western Telecommunications buy their components from Bellcrest, and they do this according to a s. ______ in order to ensure regular d. ______ On arrival the components are added to existing s. ______ held by the. company. Information concerning components delivered and issued from stock is fed into a computer, which maintains s. ______ c. ______ and can give accurate information on s. ______ l. ______ at any time. Before they bought the computer Dobson's head storeman had to count the components himself every month, which made s. ______ -t. ______ an extremely tiresome job.

3 When a new invention is made, the inventor usually a. ______ for a p. ______ to stop other people from copying his design. Once it has been t. ______ o. ______ the law protects the patent from being i. ______ by others.

Exercise B **Make sentences from these notes:**

1 Malone/tell/Jean/get/travel documents.
2 Malone/tell/Jean/make/travel arrangements/himself.
3 Downes/tell/Miss Armstrong/book/his own/hotel room.
4 Orpenshaw/tell/Malone/refuse/job.
5 Malone/tell/his secretary/take a letter.
6 Driver/tell/Downes/need extra storage space.
7 Spence/tell/Downes/be/short-term liquidity problem.
8 Malone/tell/Jean/arrange/his own/flights.
9 Malone/tell/Jean/arrange/flights.
10 Downes/tell/Miss Armstrong/telephone/Sir Frederick.

Exercise C **Complete these sentences:**

1 I look forward (hear) ______ from you.
2 We couldn't prevent them (turn to) ______ Electrovans.
3 Would you mind (wait) ______ a moment?
4 We are interested (buy) ______ 500 of your Model YZ camera.
5 I don't see the point (discuss) ______ this question at this stage.
6 These measures will enable us (increase) ______ production.
7 We are relying (receive) ______ the goods by the end of the week.
8 I haven't finished (draw up) ______ my proposals yet.
9 Did you remember (bring) ______ that report, Miss Smith?
10 You don't seem (understand) ______ what I'm saying.
11 He suggested (re-schedule) ______ our deliveries.
12 He insists (see) ______ you personally, sir.

Exercise D **Make sentences from the table below:**

Example:

a) It is important to diversify our product range.

b) Yes, but it's *__more__* *important to keep down costs.*

It	is	(more)	important	to diversify	our product range
The fire	was	(not)	essential	to halt	costs
			difficult	to increase	our position
			bad enough	to keep down	production
			serious enough	to strengthen	our sales
				to slow up	

Exercise E **Written task**

Write Dennis Evans' letter to customers setting out the consequences of the fire at Bellcrest. Use these notes:

Fire at factory

Destroyed nearly all finished goods

Delayed delivery dates

Salesman will visit/review stock position

Reassure customer of Bellcrest's ability to deliver the goods ordered

DRILLS

Drill 1 *Paul Malone is giving his secretary instructions about his journey to the Continent.*

1 Make the travel arrangements, Jean.
HE TOLD HER TO MAKE THE TRAVEL ARRANGEMENTS.

2 I'll pick up the tickets myself, Jean.
HE TOLD HER HE WOULD PICK UP THE TICKETS HIMSELF.

Drill 2 *When he returns from his tour of customers, Dennis Evans reports to Downes.*

1 Will they receive the goods on time? They're concerned about that.
I SEE. THEY'RE CONCERNED ABOUT RECEIVING THE GOODS ON TIME.

2 Their supplies mustn't be re-scheduled. They don't want that.
I SEE. THEY DON'T WANT THEIR SUPPLIES TO BE RE-SCHEDULED.

Dialogue **Making Reservations**

On one of his visits to England, Sam Urwin telephones a travel agent.

Yes, can you tell me the times of flights to Munich on the evening of the 15th, please?
Could you book me on the 5.45 flight?
No, first class, please.
Single, please.
Urwin. U-R-W-I-N.
Grand Hotel, Cononation Avenue, W.1.
There's one more thing. When should I check in?
Thank you very much. Goodbye.

Drill 3 *Dennis Evans and the Sales Representatives are discussing the effects of the fire on their customers' orders for the RN1 components.*

1 Look, Dennis, if we're going to satisfy everybody, it's obvious that we must increase production of the RN1.
THAT'S JUST THE POINT. THE FACT IS WE CAN'T INCREASE PRODUCTION OF THE RN1.

2 Well, if we cut production of the other products we could do it.
THAT'S JUST THE POINT. THE FACT IS WE CAN'T CUT PRODUCTION OF THE OTHER PRODUCTS.

Drill 4 *Tom Driver and Dennis Evans are discussing their problems after the Bellcrest fire. Evans has some ideas.*

Our immediate problem is simply to meet the orders on hand.
IT SEEMS TO ME THAT THERE ARE TWO WAYS OF MEETING THE ORDERS ON HAND.

Now listen to Evans when he makes suggestions about how to solve the problems.

Our immediate problem is simply to meet the orders on hand.
IT SEEMS TO ME THAT THERE ARE TWO WAYS OF MEETING THE ORDERS ON HAND. FIRST, BY INCREASING PRODUCTION, AND SECOND, BY RESCHEDULING DELIVERIES.

1 increase production/reschedule deliveries
2 delay some orders/reduce others
3 work overtime/take on new staff
4 explain position/guarantee new delivery dates
5 replan transport/check stock levels
6 write to them/visit them
7 review all orders on hand/consult salesmen
8 use factory space/rent other buildings

ACTIVE LISTENING

George and Harry are two executives of Western Telecommunications, one of Bellcrest's customers. They are discussing how the fire will affect their orders.

1 What reassurance has Evans given them in his letter?

. . . .

. . . .

2 What does Evans fail to mention in the letter?

. . . .

. . . .

3 Why is Western Telecommunications in a difficult position?

. . . .

. . . .

4 What does George want to know in order to judge the extent of their problem?

. . . .

. . . .

5 What is the position as regards RN2's?

. . . .

. . . .

6 Why is this?

. . . .

. . . .

7 What did Harry do as soon as he got the letter?

. . . .

. . . .

8 What does George think the purpose of Evans' visit is?

. . . .

. . . .

9 What does George hope to achieve by contacting Downes?

. . . .

. . . .

10 What does George ask Harry to consider?

. . . .

. . . .

11 What does George feel about his firm's relationship with Bellcrest?

. . . .

. . . .

12 What is Harry's attitude towards this problem?

. . . .

. . . .

ROLE SIMULATION

Statement of Problem

When all his salesmen have returned from visiting customers. Dennis Evans calls them to a meeting together with Tom Driver, the Production Manager. The problem to be discussed concerns the RN1, an electronic component in considerable demand among customers. Unfortunately, the fire destroyed all but 1500 of these components in stock, and the Production Manager maintains that he is unable to produce more than 5000 by the end of next month. The purpose of the meeting is therefore to establish how many RN1's will be required by the end of next month according to existing orders, whether customers are willing to allow their deliveries to be re-scheduled and for Dennis Evans to hear from his salesmen which customers have prior claims on available stocks.

Written follow-up You are Dennis Evans. Write a short report to Paul Malone on the decisions you have made on the basis of your meeting.

A TRIP ABROAD

On his way to visit customers and agents in Europe, Malone unexpectedly ran into Donald Williams, Managing Director of Electrovans, at the air terminal. Williams was also planning to market a speed control device for electric vehicles, similar to the SC1, and had offered a job to Orpenshaw to develop it. Malone told Williams that he knew he had offered Orpenshaw a job. Williams did not attempt to deny it, and added that he thought Orpenshaw should have a chance of continuing his work on the SC1, particularly as he understood that Bellcrest was not interested in the device. When Janet Malone unintentionally revealed that this might not be so, Williams immediately became interested. After Malone had left, he offered Janet a coffee. She accepted, and said she would give him a lift home.

The first customer Malone had to visit was M. Picard in Paris. Bellcrest's inability to deliver on time put Picard in a difficult position. He had persuaded a reluctant Board to order components from a British firm only a short time ago, and to have to admit that these would not be delivered on time would make things very unpleasant both for him and for Bellcrest. Malone had noticed that Picard's order was an extremely large one, and asked him if he really needed a thousand RN2's per month right through the summer. Picard admitted that there was some seasonal variation in his production schedules, but insisted that the transistors he had ordered were needed very urgently indeed. Malone was unable to change his mind on this point.

From Paris Malone flew on to Munich, where he visited some customers and then met Walter Heinlein, Bellcrest's agent in Germany. During the course of their conversation, the question of the SC1 was brought up. Heinlein rather surprisingly wanted to know whether Bellcrest would be willing to sell him the patents in Germany. He said that he thought that there was now a market for an AC speed control device, although there hadn't been five years ago when the SC1 was suspended. Malone was naturally very interested by what Heinlein had to say, and more so when he was told that the D.A.U. company were putting a lot of money into developing a small electric town car. He told Heinlein he would like to follow this up, and Heinlein promised that a meeting would be arranged with D.A.U's Technical Director.

Later that Evening Malone telephoned Janet, who was still worried about speaking out of turn to Donald Williams at the air terminal. When she assured him that she had given away nothing about the SC1 to Williams, Malone told her it didn't matter.

Then next day, Malone visited Dr Lang, Bellcrest's largest customer in Germany. Once again he had to explain the effects of the fire on Bellcrest's delivery schedules and apologize for the inevitable delays. Dr Lang had placed one order which could not be delayed, and that was for a consignment of 4,500 resistors for his model P 43. Although Malone thought it would not be easy to meet this order, he agreed to do what he could.

Dr Lang went on to mention that he had not received his previous consignment of resistors. Heinlein was contacted and he said that the resistors had been in Munich for a week, but had been delayed in the Customs. He added that Dr Lang would receive the resistors that afternoon or the following morning.

Malone then brought up the question of the remainder of Dr Lang's order for the following month, most of which was for components for Dr Lang's AM17 model. Malone found that these were no longer needed, as Dr Lang's company had developed a smaller, cheaper model. These components were, however, exactly those needed by Picard in Paris, so Malone immediately agreed to take 5000 off Dr Lang's hands.

Before he left for Copenhagen, Malone met Heinlein again, who had contacted Picard and arranged to despatch the components to Paris immediately. Heinlein also told Malone that he had been in touch with Dr Mandl, D.A.U.'s Technical Director, and a meeting had been arranged for that afternoon. He had some disturbing news for Malone too. Dr Mandl had told Heinlein that he had had a visitor from another British company, which was developing a speed control device similar to the SC1. Malone guessed that the company was Electrovans and the visitor Donald Williams.

Malone was right. When Williams returned from Europe, he went to Ashburnham's Bank. He promised Sir Frederick that he would send the Bank Electrovans' report on a speed control device the following week. He also told Sir Frederick and Needham that he thought Malone was trying to revive the SC1.

EXERCISES

xercise A

1 When Malone visited Paris he found Picard d. at Bellcrest's inability to deliver according to schedule. Picard a. Bellcrest's difficulties, but as the delay put him in an u. position, he insisted that the components he had ordered were needed u. .H. for Malone, Dr Lang was only too p. to return five thousand of the components Picard needed. This was 1. for Malone, and he was very g. to Dr Lang, as he would have lost Picard's custom if he hadn't been able to meet his order.

2 Malone couldn't understand why Dr Lang's order had been delayed as it had been d. from England by a. f. a month previously. He therefore telephoned his a. , Heinlein. Heinlein told him that the c. had not been c. by Customs, as Bellcrest had not sent sufficient copies of the i. . He also told Malone that he was arranging for Picard's order to be sent on by his f. a. to Paris.

Exercise B

Here are some notes Malone has made reminding him what he will have to do during the day.

Write full sentences using 'when', 'before' or 'until':

Examples:

Phone Needham – make appointment.
I'll have to make an appointment when I phone Needham.

Adjuster coming – look at policy first
I'll have to look at the policy before the adjuster comes.

Check stock list – delay seeing Driver until then.
I'll have to delay seeing Driver until I check the stock list.

1 Seeing Spence – look though file first.
2 Buyer coming – negotiate contract.
3 Speak Driver – think about production of SC1 first.
4 Lunch with Downes – leave RN2 question until then.
5 Janet phoning – book theatre tickets first.
6 Attend meeting – read agenda first.
7 Ring Urwin – invite to dinner.
8 Write SC1 report – review past developments.
9 Visit M. P. Consultants – brief Evans first.
10 Urwin coming to dinner – keep quiet about Orpenshaw until then.

Exercise C

Complete the sentences from the notes:

Example:
Picard/informed/Malone/his firm/require a thousand RN2s.
Picard informed Malone that his firm required a thousand RN2s.

1 Urwin/admitted/Malone/he/find Williams very interesting.
2 Spence/warned/the Committee/the Insurance Company/not meet the claim immediately.

3 Malone/explained/Janet/Bellcrest/must keep quiet about the SC1.
4 M.P. Consultants/told/Bellcrest/they think/now a market for the SC1.
5 Spence/pointed out/Downes/the Bank/not know anything about the developme plans.
6 Janet/mentioned/her husband/Williams/want to find out about the SC1.
7 Evans/assured/his customers/Bellcrest/increase production as soon as possible.
8 Heinlein/informed/Malone/the D.A.U. Company/expanding fast.
9 Orpenshaw/warned/Malone/Electrovans/intend to produce a speed control device.
10 Dr Lang/told/Malone/his firm/not require the ZA24 transistors.

Exercise D Complete these sentences:

Malone: Unfortunately most of our stocks (destroy) ______ last week when a fire (break) ______ out in our factory.

Lang: Yes, I (hear) ______ about it. Several European countries (buy) ______ regularly from Bellcrest and your products (value) ______ in Germany. The fire (report) ______ in our newspapers.

Malone: Some of the reports in the English papers (exaggerate) ______ the extent of the damage. They (not mention) ______ that production (increase) ______ in the near future. Of course, deliveries (delay) ______ to a certain extent.

Lang: Actually, at the moment I am more worried about our last order from Bellcrest. The consignment (expect) ______ about 3 weeks ago but it (fail) ______ to arrive up to now.

Malone: That's very strange. It (air freight) ______ on the second of the month. I (speak) ______ to our agent about it immediately and I hope the matter (settle) ______ to your satisfaction.

Exercise E Written Task

a *You are Paul Malone. Send a telegram to Picard, saying:*
1 His components are being sent immediately from Germany.
2 The forwarding agent is Dupierre of Paris.
3 He will inform Picard of their arrival.
4 He can expect them by the end of the week.
5 A letter is following.

b *Now write the letter to Picard confirming your telegram.*

DRILLS

Drill 1 I'll answer that question but I'm going to speak to Malone first.
OH, I SEE. YOU'RE GOING TO SPEAK TO MALONE BEFORE YOU ANSWER THAT QUESTION.

I'll see Picard soon and then I'll reassure him.
OH, I SEE. YOU'LL REASSURE PICARD WHEN YOU SEE HIM.

Spence is going to write a report, and we'll wait until then.
OH, I SEE. YOU'LL WAIT UNTIL SPENCE WRITES A REPORT.

Drill 2 Oh, I agree it is most unfortunate about the fire.
EVANS AGREED THAT IT WAS MOST UNFORTUNATE ABOUT THE FIRE.

I must admit that Bellcrest won't be able to supply you immediately.
EVANS ADMITTED THAT BELLCREST WOULDN'T BE ABLE TO SUPPLY HIM IMMEDIATELY.

Drill 3 *Malone is showing some visitors round the factory and is answering their questions.*

When did you build this factory?
IT WAS BUILT IN 1957.

Where do you keep your surplus stocks?
THEY ARE KEPT IN OUR WAREHOUSE.

Will you export these goods?
YES, THEY WILL BE EXPORTED TO EUROPE.

1 In 1957
2 In our warehouse
3 To Europe
4 Next week
5 Our Sales Manager

6 Our Chief Engineer
7 All electrically driven vehicles
8 About five years ago

Dialogue **At the Air Terminal**

Paul Malone is returning from Europe. His plane has just landed at Heathrow Airport.

Yes, I am.
Yes, of course.
No, only three days.
Oh, only in Europe. Germany, France and Denmark, actually.
Thank you.
Nothing, actually. I've been on a business trip, not a holiday.
Oh, I see.
No, nothing. I went to the wrong gate, that's all.
No, nothing.

Drill 4 *Malone is talking to Bellcrest's agent in Italy. The agent has a number of requests. Malone thinks these will be difficult to meet. However, he is prepared to offer something.*

I believe we could sell a lot more for you if you would agree to reduce prices by 10%.
IT WOULD BE VERY DIFFICULT TO REDUCE THEM BY 10%, I'M AFRAID, BUT THERE'S A GOOD CHANCE OF REDUCING THEM BY 5%.

1 5%
2 £3,000
3 the end of the month
4 2000 copies
5 2 men
6 10 days
7 the beginning of September
8 a maximum of 20%

Drill 5 *Malone has now telephoned to Downes and told him about the agent's requests. Downes agrees with Malone's reactions.*

Malone is now talking to the agent again and confirming what he said earlier.

I asked if you could reduce prices by 10%.
UNFORTUNATELY WE CAN'T REDUCE THEM BY 10%, BUT ALL BEING WELL, WE SHOULD BE ABLE TO REDUCE THEM BY 5%.

Notice that Malone is still being cautious about what he promises:
'*All being well,* we *should* be able to . . . .'

1 5%
2 £3,000
3 the end of the month
4 2,000 copies
5 2 men
6 10 days
7 the beginning of September
8 a maximum of 20%
9 the end of next week.

ACTIVE LISTENING

During his visit to Germany Malone meets Dr Mandl, the Technical Director of D.A.U. They are discussing their interest in the automotive field.

1 What is the purpose of Malone's visit to Germany?

. . . .

. . . .

2 What has Dr Mandl been working on?

. . . .

. . . .

3 What reason does Mandl give for being interested in this field?

. . . .

. . . .

4 What do both men think will happen before long?

. . . .

. . . .

5 Why does Malone think there are good prospects for electrically driven cars?

. . . .

. . . .

6 What is the main problem in the development of such cars?

. . . .

. . . .

7 What will be the advantage of Bellcrest's device?

. . . .

. . . .

8 Give two reasons why Malone cannot give Mandl more detailed information about the SC1.

. . . .

. . . .

9 Why is Malone so interested in Mandl's reactions, do you think?

. . . .

. . . .

10 What important information does Malone get from Mandl?

. . . .

. . . .

11 Why is Mandl going to London?

. . . .

. . . .

12 Why does Malone want him to visit Bellcrest?

. . . .

ROLE SIMULATION

Statement of Problem

Despite the fire, Bellcrest's work had to go on as normally as was possible in the circumstances. A meeting had been arranged two months before between interested parties in Bellcrest and a visiting Japanese delegation from the House of Kakubishi.

The House of Kakubishi are interested in becoming sole agents in Japan for Bellcrest's RN, BX, HJ, GJ and LX range of components. (The X ranges are transistors, the J ranges are resistors). Japan is a country in which Bellcrest does not yet have an agent. Bellcrest is in principle interested in having an agent in Japan, as they feel there is a potential market of some size for their products in that country.

The Japanese have spent the morning touring Bellcrest and after lunch the two delegations meet to discuss the whole question of the House of Kakubishi's proposed agency for Bellcrest products. It has already been agreed in principle between Downes and Yamaguchi, Managing Director of the House of Kakubishi, that nothing stands in the way of co-operation, subject to other questions being satisfactorily settled. The outstanding problems, among others, to be settled at the meeting are those of deliveries, servicing, product range, or routines, sales literature, advertising, terms and methods of payment and commission.

You should re-enact this meeting.

Written follow-up

Both sides should write a letter confirming the agreements made at the meeting.

STUDYING THE MARKET

After Donald Williams' visit to the Bank, Sir Frederick and Needham discussed whether to support Bellcrest or Electrovans. Needham felt that Electrovans was more adventurous than Bellcrest. Sir Frederick agreed with this, but felt that Bellcrest was sounder than Electrovans. He pointed out that Electrovans was still very dependent on one or two big customers: 45% of Electrovans' business went to one company, Beamish Motors, for example. Needham had to agree with this, although he still believed that Electrovans was more forward-looking than Bellcrest. Sir Frederick, however, was not prepared to make up his mind which company to invest in.

Malone returned from Europe and reported back to Downes. Downes was not at all happy about Dr Mandl's visit to Bellcrest, in spite of the fact that D.A.U. represented a potential customer for the SC1. Malone pointed out that although D.A.U. was only a potential customer, this was the first direct contact Bellcrest had had with a vehicle manufacturer. He felt that this was a great opportunity which should not be overlooked. Downes conceded the point as it was too late to put Dr Mandl off.

Downes went on to tell Malone that there was to be a Board meeting in ten days' time, and that the SC1 was bound to be mentioned. Although there wasn't time enough to circulate a complete report before the meeting, he wanted as much information from the market survey as possible.

Malone went at once to Orpenshaw, who at first didn't want to see him or any visitors, as he had a lot of work to do on the SC1. Malone reminded him that Dr Mandl was coming. Orpenshaw was quite happy to see Dr Mandl, as he felt that Mandl would be more interested in the SC1 as a piece of engineering than anyone else. Malone asked him whether he had any test results ready, and told him that he needed as much information as possible in three days' time. Orpenshaw was disgusted at only having three days, but said he would do what he could.

When Dr Mandl arrived, Malone introduced him to Orpenshaw, who got on extremely well with him. Orpenshaw was careful to explain only what the SC1 did, not how it worked, and Dr Mandl had plenty of questions to ask him. When, at the end of his visit, Orpenshaw took Dr Mandl to see Downes, he said he liked the SC1 very much. Although he said Orpenshaw had asked him more questions than he had asked Orpenshaw, he told Downes that he had learned all he needed to know about the SC1. He had thought of visiting another company to discuss speed controls, but that would no longer be necessary.

Although he would have preferred to stay with Dr Mandl, Malone had to go up to London with Evans to see M.P. Consultants and hear the results of their preliminary study.

M.P. Consultants hadn't really had enough time to prepare their study. When Malone arrived, Sherwood and Dean, Dr Perkins' assistants, started to run through the data they had collected. They showed him some statistics on a screen, including a chart showing the growth in production over the past twenty years: total electric vehicle production had risen from 3,450 to 18,000 a year during this period. Malone interrupted to say that as all this information was contained in their report he would prefer not to go through it now but concentrate on details that affected the SC1.

Sherwood and Dean were not able to give him much detailed information. They had found out that most electronic control systems at present in use were fairly simple, whereas the SC1 was not. They had sent questionnaires to vehicle manufacturers, who indicated that the SC1 would only be of interest to them if it enabled them to offer a more attractive product for their customers to buy than their present power systems. They had also questioned the customers, and their research indicated that 55% would welcome the increased mileage a device like the SC1 would offer, as long as there was no increase in cost to achieve it, whereas only 25% felt that increased mileage was worth paying for. These findings were not particularly encouraging for Malone.

Dr Perkins added that they had also questioned potential users of electric vehicles but, to Malone's disappointment, had only had time to include some of their preliminary findings in their report.

Dr Perkins went on to discuss car manufacturers, most of whom seemed to be more aware of the disadvantages of battery-driven cars than of the advantages. All car manufacturers were agreed on the requirements of small cars for cities. These were small size, simple operation, good manoeuvrability, minimum pollution and low cost. Malone pointed out that an electric car suited these requirements and that the SC1 went a long way towards solving one of its main drawbacks: its short range. Dr Perkins said they hoped to cover the smaller manufacturers more thoroughly in the next stage of their research, as at the moment they only had rumours, not hard facts. She mentioned a rumour that Cremorne Cars had already thought of developing an electric city car, but had dropped the project as they had not been able to persuade an electronics firm to develop the right kind of speed control. Cremorne Cars had refused to confirm the rumour, and their name was not mentioned in M.P. Consultants' report. Malone asked Dr Perkins to take the matter up with them again without mentioning Bellcrest's name.

Electrovans had by now submitted their report on their AC speed control to Ashburnham's Bank. Sir Frederick was impressed by the report, but despite Needham's enthusiasm for Electrovans he insisted on waiting for Bellcrest's report before making any decision about the Bank's loan.

EXERCISES

Exercise A **Complete the following sentences:**

1 Ashburnham and Needham discussed whether to support Bellcrest or Electrovans. Needham felt that Electrovans were more a. than Bellcrest, and that the company was a f. -1. concern. Williams, he said, had p. a. with development whereas Downes had been more cautious. Sir Frederick felt that Electrovans l. the s. of Bellcrest and were too d. on one or two large customers. Needham replied that that was the reason why Williams wanted capital to b. f. and f. e. . Without this capital, he couldn't a. to.

2 When Malone visited M.P. Consultants he was shown some s on the d. Sherwood and Dean had collected. The s. showed the principal manufacturers of electric vehicles and their v. of p. .Malone was shown a c. on a screen indicating the g. in production and the t. p. of electric vehicles over the past twenty years. To get this information, M.P. Consultants had sent q. to vehicle manufacturers. A lot of the data on potential customers was not included in their p. s. , as the p. f. were outside its s.

Exercise B **Write sentences from the following notes:**

Examples:
Make/our own enquiries/cheap/commission a survey.
Making our own enquiries is cheaper than commissioning a survey.

Develop/project/interesting/sell/products.
Developing a project is more interesting than selling products.

1 Live/home/comfortable/stay/second-rate hotel.
2 Pay/high insurance premium/good/lose/a lot/money.
3 Make/statement/simple/give interviews.
4 Meet/orders/satisfactory/ask/customers/accept delays.
5 Soak/papers/water/bad/burn/them.
6 Make/components/ourselves/expensive/buy/Bellcrest.
7 Finance/new developments/progressive/look for/quick profits.
8 Find/markets/hard/plan/production.
9 Approach/potential customers/adventurous/wait/them/approach/us.
10 Commission/survey/safe/listen/rumours.

Exercise C **Complete the sentences using 'much', 'many', 'a lot of' and 'more':**

Perkins: We sent out questionnaires to firms that already use electric vehicles.
Malone: Did of them reply?

Perkins:	About 40%, which is quite compared with other surveys. than half of these companies felt that there would not be advantage in increased mileage if this raised the cost of the vehicle. Only 25% of them felt it would be worth paying for increased mileage.
Malone:	25%! That's not
Perkins:	I'm afraid we haven't been able to find out about potential users of electric vehicles although we questioned companies in the private vehicle sector. There seems to be interest abroad than in the U.K. I think you would get quite support from European companies. But at the moment there are not British manufacturers interested in developing an electric car. Of course there have been rumours that Cremorne Cars tried to develop an electric city car but dropped the project because they couldn't get the right kind of AC speed control. Unfortunately, they won't confirm these rumours, so we haven't to go on in the way of hard facts. However, we will try to get information about this.

Exercise D *Sir Frederick and Needham are discussing whether to support Bellcrest or Electrovans.*

Complete the following sentences, using 'while', 'although', 'in spite of' and 'whereas':

Example:
Needham didn't like Downes, although *he admitted he was a good businessman.*

Sir Frederick:	Downes is a sound businessman his reluctance to take risks. I know he abandoned a lot of development projects getting Bellcrest back on its feet

again, but this was necessary if the company was to remain in business. And he did a very good job, forcing Williams to resign was perhaps a mistake. Downes has increased profits   still maintaining a high level of technical excellence. Bellcrest sell to a wide range of customers   Electrovans is still very dependent on one company for their trade.

Needham: Well, Sir Frederick,   I agree wholeheartedly with what you say, I think you have perhaps overlooked one or two points. Williams has the full backing of his staff   Downes has lost the support of some of his technical staff. Men like Orpenshaw don't like to see their projects abandoned even   they may appreciate the financial reasons for such measures. In fact it is quite possible that Orpenshaw may transfer to Electrovans   this has not been settled yet. If he leaves Bellcrest, the company will find it difficult to develop this speed control   having produced the original designs.

Exercise E **Written Task**

Cremorne Cars was one of the manufacturers that received a questionnaire from M. P. Consultants. The Managing Director of the company, K.C.Y., passed this on to his Marketing Manager, D.B., with an accompanying memo. Write this memo for him. Use these notes:

just received
to our advantage to fill it in
draw your attention Question 6
advantages of AC speed control?
which firm has commissioned this survey?

DRILLS

Drill 1 We're getting the research done by management consultants but I don't know how quick they are.
GETTING THE RESEARCH DONE BY MANAGEMENT CONSULTANTS IS QUICKER THAN DOING IT OURSELVES, DON'T YOU THINK?

We must increase production of the BX10 and I don't know how difficult this is.
INCREASING PRODUCTION OF THE BX10 IS MORE DIFFICULT THAN RESCHEDULING THE ORDERS, DON'T YOU THINK?

I've received a little information but I don't know how good it is.
RECEIVING A LITTLE INFORMATION IS BETTER THAN RECEIVING NONE, DON'T YOU THINK?

1 quick/do/it/ourselves
2 difficult/reschedule/orders
3 good/receive/none
4 important/listen/rumours
5 easy/persuade/Bank/extend/loan
6 urgent/go on with/technical developments
7 bad/damage/warehouse
8 appropriate/concern/ourselves/industrial sector

Drill 2 Do you do any business with French companies?
NO, NOT MUCH REALLY, BUT WE DO A LOT OF BUSINESS WITH GERMAN COMPANIES.

Have you any contacts in Norway?
NO, NOT MANY REALLY, BUT WE HAVE A LOT OF CONTACTS IN SWEDEN.

1 German companies
2 Sweden
3 petrochemicals
4 surge diverters
5 research and development
6 prices
7 labour
8 industrial vehicle sector

Drill 3 60% of our customers are completely satisfied.
DOES THAT MEAN THAT 40% OF THEM ARE COMPLETEY DISSATISFIED?

Two thirds of the directors supported the project.
DOES THAT MEAN THAT ONE THIRD OF THEM OPPOSED IT?

Dialogue **At the Air Terminal.**
Dr Mandl is flying back from Heathrow to Munich.

I'm on flight 642 to Munich. This is the right check-in desk, isn't it?
Yes, one minute. Ah, here we are.
I give that up at the departure gate, don't I?
Yes, this overnight case and a briefcase.
Not at all. They're not overweight, I hope.
Yes, here it is.
No, only a few days, actually.
Oh, of course. There we are.
Oh, yes. One minute, it's locked. I've got the key here. Here it is.
My overcoat?
Oh, I see.
Thank you very much.

Drill 4 *Dr Mary Perkins of M.P. Consultants, and Brian Dean, her assistant, are discussing the advantages of electric city cars and of the SC1.*

Of course, electricity is cheap.
YES, IT CERTAINLY *IS* CHEAP, AND WHAT'S MORE, IT'S AVAILABLE EVERYWHERE.

1 available everywhere
2 easy to park
3 quiet
4 easier to drive
5 cheap to service
6 increases battery life
7 not heavy
8 time for lunch

Drill 5 *Paul Malone is at M.P. Consultants. Jim Sherwood is talking about the preliminary market study. Malone feels the information is too general. He keeps interrupting and asking for more specific information. He is rather annoyed.*

Our investigations show that the market for electric vehicles is growing, and . . .

EXCUSE ME, MR. SHERWOOD. WE *KNOW* THAT THE MARKET FOR ELECTRIC VEHICLES IS GROWING. WHAT WE WANT TO KNOW IS *HOW FAST* IT'S GROWING.

1 how fast?
2 by whom?
3 how much?
4 by whom?
5 *which* airports?
6 how many?
7 *how* soon?
8 when?

ACTIVE LISTENING

The Managing Director and the Marketing Manager of Cremorne Cars are discussing a letter they have received from M.P. Consultants.

1 What do M. P. Consultants want?

. . . .

. . . .

2 How had they dealt with the first letter?

. . . .

. . . .

3 What is Fred's reaction to this letter?

. . . .

. . . .

4 Why would Cremorne Cars be interested in the development of an AC speed control?

. . . .

. . . .

5 What reasons does Fred give for thinking that the enquiry does not originate from Bellcrest?

. . . .

. . . .

6 What does Fred think of Downes?

. . . .

. . . .

7 Who does Fred think must be employing the consultants?

. . . .

. . . .

8 If his guess is correct, why would this be bad for Cremorne Cars?

. . . .

. . . .

9 Why can't they find out if their guess is correct?

10 What does the Managing Director decide to do?

11 Why will the Managing Director write a covering letter?

12 What does Fred suggest that they should do?

ROLE SIMULATION

Statement of Problem

When Dr Mandl returned to D.A.U. in Germany he submitted an extremely enthusiastic report on the SC1, strongly recommending that it be used in D.A.U.'s projected electric vehicles. He managed to convince his Managing Director to buy from Bellcrest and shortly afterwards four representatives of D.A.U. arrived in Leicester with a view to enquiring as to Bellcrest's production plans and schedules and obtaining an estimate.

As D.A.U. propose to start manufacturing their electric vehicles within a year, they are naturally anxious to tie Bellcrest down to delivery dates and quantities as far as is possible.

The D.A.U. representatives arrived in England last night, and today they are to come to Bellcrest. Re-enact their meeting.

Written follow-up

Write a letter to either Bellcrest or D.A.U. confirming any agreements or proposals made at the meeting.

AGENDA AND MINUTES

Ashburnham had still not made up his mind whether to support Electrovans or Bellcrest. He had discussed the question with Needham. All relevant. information on their project had already been sent by Electrovans, but nothing definite had been heard from Bellcrest. All the information on the SC1 that was available had been supplied by Donald Williams. Ashburnham therefore decided to telephone Downes himself with a view to finding out what Bellcrest's plans were.

When Sir Frederick rang, Downes was most unwilling to reveal anything. Sir Frederick said he was prepared to extend Bellcrest's deadline by a month, although it would be useful to have some information before then. Downes answered that both the Bank and the Board of Directors would be given full details as soon as they became available. The next Board meeting was in a week's time, and the Bank's loan would certainly be discussed. Sir Frederick was obliged to accept this and Downes had succeeded in revealing nothing about the SC1. When Downes rang off, Needham said that at least the question of the Bank's loan would be on the agenda of the next Board meeting and that this might help him in getting more information about the SC1.

When Downes had finished talking to Sir Frederick, he rang up Paul Malone about the market study from M.P. Consultants. He told Malone he didn't like it, as he didn't think the findings would persuade the Board of Directors to back the SC1. Malone protested that the study only showed the preliminary findings and that the general picture was much brighter. He mentioned D.A.U. and Cremorne Cars as potential customers, but Downes dismissed these as rumours, not hard facts. Malone said he would see whether he could get any definite information about Cremorne Cars' interest and would let Downes know.

Malone immediately rang up Dr Perkins, but she was unable to supply any further information, at least none that could be put on paper. Malone was extremely disappointed. When Downes heard this, he said that the SC1 could not now be discussed at the next Board meeting as the case for backing the SC1 was not good enough. He told Malone to get his report ready for circulation by the 20th August instead.

At that point Spence came in to show Downes the revised agenda for the coming Board meeting. Spence was surprised to hear that Downes no longer wanted to discuss the SC1 at the meeting. In order to avoid giving Needham any chance of bringing up the subject, Downes changed the wording of item four on the agenda from 'To consider development projects in connection with the loan from Ashburnham's Bank' to 'To consider suggested repayment of the Ashburnham Bank loan'. Spence wondered whether Downes was not being overcautious, because as far as they both knew, Needham was unaware of the proposal to revive the SC1. Downes felt, however, that if he was given the chance Needham would press for details of the project and suggested that Spence should look up the minutes of the meeting at which the SC1 was suspended five years before.

At the Board meeting, Downes stated that the Company could not afford to lose the Bank's support. The Bank's position was confirmed by Needham, who said that the loan would only be continued if Bellcrest showed evidence of worthwhile development projects. Downes admitted that a major project was being considered, but declined to go into details. Needham, then said that it was rumoured that Bellcrest was thinking of reviving the SC1, a project that had been axed five years before.

Downes replied that he was concerned that a Director had heard a rumour and had failed to inform the management of the company. He asked Needham to have a word with him about the source of the rumour after the meeting. He was forced, however, to admit that the SC1 was being considered for development, but said that a full report would not be tabled until the next Board meeting.

Needham persisted. He asked why revival of the SC1 was necessary when it had been rejected five years before. Downes replied that it had been suspended, not rejected, and Spence confirmed this by looking up the minutes of the Board meeting of 3rd March, 1966. Unfortunately, March, one of the Directors, remembered the sentence that followed this in the minutes, which said that it had been resolved that the possibility of selling the patents and designs to another company should be considered. The discussion was continued.

After the meeting Downes had a word with Needham. He told Needham that he knew the Bank didn't like having to wait another month for a full discussion on development plans, but that he always insisted on decisions being taken on the basis of adequate information. Adequate information on the SC1 was not yet to hand. He went on to ask Needham where he had picked up the rumour that the SC1 was being revived, to which Needham replied that the wife of one of his senior executives had been rather indiscreet. Downes assumed this was Janet Malone and told Paul Malone.

On their way to the theatre that evening, Paul Malone brought this up with his wife. Janet angrily insisted that she did not know Needham. She suggested that Donald Williams might have told Needham. When Malone refused to believe this, she lost her temper, got out of the car and went home.

EXERCISES

Exercise A **Complete the following sentences:**

1 Downes told Malone that the findings of the preliminary survey did not s. him. As the findings did not c. him, he felt that the study would not be enough to p. the Board to back the SC1. He said he needed h. f. to p. to the Board, not r. . He added that the facts and figures in the survey were not s. on their own, and asked Malone to prepare a full report for c. by 20th August.

2 Spence brought the a. for the next Board meeting in to Downes. As Downes didn't want to discuss the SC1, the w. of i. four had to be r. . Downes did this so that Needham would have no chance of r. the s. of the SC1, and pressing for d. of the project. He also told Spence to look up the m. of the meeting at which the SC1 had been suspended in case he was unable to keep Needham off the s. of development projects.

3 When Needham raised the subject of the SC1 at the Board meeting, Downes confirmed that a major project was u. c. . He said he intended to s. his management's r. at the next Board meeting, when he hoped to be able to t. a full r. on the project. A more important i. to Downes was the source of the rumour Needham had heard.

4 Downes told Needham that the SC1 had been suspended five years before, not rejected, and Spence confirmed this by looking up the r. m. . Mr. March said, however, that Spence was q. parts of a document o. of c. as the following sentence recommended that the patents and designs should be sold.

Exercise B **Complete these sentences:**

When Downes realized that Bellcrest's loan (reconsider) by the Bank, he called a meeting of the management committee to discuss plans for diversification. The SC1 (choose) as the most promising new product. This device (invent) by Bob Orpenshaw several years before but the project (suspend) because of financial difficulties. There had been quite a controversy over the matter and Donald Williams, the Marketing Manager, (oblige) to resign because of it. Downes did not want to reveal Bellcrest's renewed interest in the SC1 until a market survey (carry out) by a firm of management consultants.

At the moment, this study (conduct) by M.P. Consultants. A preliminary survey (just complete) from the answers to questionnaires which (send out) some weeks previously. Downes (now see) this survey. He found it disappointing and decided not to mention the SC1 to the Board of Directors, although he (continually press) by the Bank to give them details of his development plans. M. P. Consultants (ask) to investigate rumours that Cremorne Cars are interested in manufacturing an electric car, and at the moment further enquiries (make)

Exercise C *These are some of the notes Miss Armstrong took at the last Board meeting.* **Using these notes, write complete sentences as they would appear in the minutes. Follow the pattern given in the example:**

decide/suspend/SC1.
It was decided *to suspend the SC1.*

1 Resolve/abandon/work/BX10.
2 Suggest/all development projects/review.
3 Decide/postpone/discussion/SC1/next meeting.
4 Assume/full report/ready/August 20th.
5 The Chairman/request/table/full report/SC1.
6 SC1/consider/too expensive.
7 Increase/Directors' fees/approve.
8 The Directors/request/be/more punctual.
9 Resolve/diversify/product range/within the near future.
10 Next meeting/arrange/September 2nd.

Exercise D **Complete the sentences:**

Examples:
Downes did not want to go to the trouble (inform) the Board.
Downes did not want to go to the trouble of informing the Board.

He was unwilling (raise) the matter.
He was unwilling to raise the matter.

Bellcrest had revived the SC1 project with a view (diversify) their product range. Electrovans were also interested (market) a speed control device similar to the SC1. Both companies were eager (get) financial support from Ashburnham's Bank. Donald Williams, the Managing Director of Electrovans, had already drawn up proposals (develop) his product and he took every opportunity (present) his case to Sir Frederick Ashburnham. Maurice Downes, on the other hand, insisted (treat) Bellcrest's project as confidential. He maintained that there was no point (discuss) the plans until detailed information was available. Sir Frederick was unwilling (decide) which firm to support. His assistant, Edward Needham, thought there was a good case (invest) in Electrovans and he persisted (draw) Sir Frederick's attention to the advantages (support) Williams. However, Sir Frederick was not prepared (commit) himself.

Exercise E **Written Task**

Charles Spence has to send out letters to members of the Board confirming arrangements for the next meeting. Minutes of the previous meeting and agenda are also enclosed. Write this letter for Spence. Use these notes:

1 time, date and place of next meeting.
2 enclosures.
3 agenda.
4 of special importance: renewal of bank loan.

DRILLS

Drill 1 *Two executives from a motor manufacturer's are discussing recent developments in the automotive field.*

Was Donald Williams trying to find out about Bellcrest?
YES, BUT HE WASN'T THE ONLY ONE. QUESTIONS WERE BEING ASKED BY EDWARD NEEDHAM AS WELL.

Are Bellcrest working on an AC speed control?
YES, BUT THEY AREN'T THE ONLY ONES. THAT DEVICE IS BEING DEVELOPED BY ELECTROVANS AS WELL.

1 questions/ask/Edward Needham
2 that device/develop/Electrovans
3 interest/show/private vehicle sector
4 electric cars/design/British firm
5 potential users/question/consultants
6 the market/study/Electrovans
7 a contract/negotiate/Passlee Electronics
8 Williams' proposals/considered/Sir Frederick

Drill 2 *Sir Keith Frisby, a member of Bellcrest's Board of Directors, was absent from a meeting of the Board. After the meeting he rings Downes to ask him what was decided.*

Did you decide anything about new projects?
YES, IT WAS DECIDED TO REVIEW NEW PROJECTS.

And the SC1? Did you resolve to continue with it?
NO, IT WAS RESOLVED THAT THE SC1 SHOULD BE SUSPENDED.

1 yes/decided/to/review
2 no/resolved/that/suspended
3 no/suggested/that/abandoned
4 no/proposed/that/not/sold
5 no/decided/not/to abandon/completely
6 yes/suggested/that/maintained
7 no/proposed/that/continue
8 yes/agreed/that/approached

Drill 3 *Malone is talking to Orpenshaw about the problem of support for the SC1.*

The Bank may finance Electrovans. Needham considers it has a case.
I SEE. NEEDHAM CONSIDERS THE BANK HAS A CASE FOR FINANCING ELECTROVANS.

Downes isn't giving them any information. He's very unwilling.
I SEE. HE'S VERY UNWILLING TO GIVE THEM ANY INFORMATION.

Dialogue **Asking for information**
Paul Malone rings up Dr Perkins to ask for more information on potential customers.

HELLO	DR PERKINS?
	Is that Dr Perkins?

I WANTED TO	TAKE UP	THE
I wonder if I could	raise	
I'd like to		

MATTER OF CREMORNE CARS.	IS IT POSSIBLE TO
question	Can you
	Are you able to
	Are you in a position to

GIVE ME	ANY MORE INFORMATION?	I REALLY DO NEED
let me have	further	I'm very anxious to get

SOME	HARD	FACTS	TO PRESENT TO	MY	BOARD.
	concrete	information	to put before		
	reliable				

THAT'S A PITY.
That's very unfortunate.
That's rather awkward.

I QUITE UNDERSTAND.
Yes, I see your point.

I'D BE MOST GRATEFUL IF YOU COULD.
I'd appreciate it

NOT AT THE MOMENT, THANK YOU. GOODBYE, DR PERKINS.
Not just now,

Drill 4 *Maurice Downes and Charles Spence are talking informally in Downes's office. Notice how Spence 'picks up' a subject mentioned by Downes, in order to raise a matter he wants to talk about.*

By the way, I see that there's still a lot of overtime being worked.
I'M GLAD YOU MENTIONED OVERTIME. I WANTED TO TAKE UP THE MATTER OF TEMPORARY STAFF.

1 temporary staff
2 Heinlein's expenses
3 Mandl's visit
4 fee for M. P. Consultants
5 agenda (for Board meeting)
6 Orpenshaw's contract
7 agreement with Passlee Electronics
8 Miss Armstrong's salary

Drill 5 *Charles Spence is attending the weekly management meeting. Downes is Chairman. Look at Spence's copy of the agenda. On it he has made notes of some small points he wants to make, and questions he wants to ask.*

AGENDA

1 Minutes of last meeting (Can we receive copies earlier?)
2 Matters arising
  i) Heinlein's expenses (I have written to him as requested)
  ii) Fee for M. P. Consultants (Has the fee been agreed?)
  iii) Temporary staff (How many are we employing?)
3 Trading account to 30 June (Does not include sales to Japan)
4 Market survey (When can we expect full report?)
5 Insurance (Our claim has been accepted by the insurance company)
6 Any other business (Can we meet an hour earlier next week?)

Now, any comments on the minutes of the last meeting, Charles?
AS FAR AS I'M CONCERNED, I'D JUST LIKE TO ASK IF WE COULD RECEIVE COPIES EARLIER?

Then there's the matter of Heinlein's expenses. You have something on this I believe, Charles?
AS FAR AS I'M CONCERNED, I'D JUST LIKE TO SAY THAT I HAVE WRITTEN TO HIM, AS REQUESTED.

ACTIVE LISTENING

Mr Birley, who works for one of London's leading merchant banks, is being interviewed about the functions of a merchant bank.

1 What kinds of problems does a merchant bank solve?

....

....

2 To what extent is a merchant bank a lending organization?

....

....

3 What sort of financial advice can a merchant bank give a company?

....

....

4 If a company wants to borrow from a merchant bank, what must it do?

....

....

5 How does the bank satisfy itself that this is the case?

....

....

6 What does the bank usually want in return for the loan?

....

....

7 Why does the bank insist on having security for the loan?

....

....

8 Why is this sort of business attractive to a merchant bank?

....

....

9 What does a merchant bank hope will happen?

....

....

10 At what stage does a merchant bank withdraw its financial support and what happens then?

....

....

11 In what ways will a merchant bank try to influence the development of a company?

....

....

12 What is the ultimate objective of the merchant bank?

....

....

ROLE SIMULATION

atement of Problem

Paul Malone feels that sooner or later Downes or the Board of Directors will ask him exactly how he proposes to market the SC1. The product is outside Bellcrest's established field, which will mean looking for new customers in new industries, such as the industrial and commercial vehicle sectors. Bellcrest has no reputation for such devices as the SC1, and suitable advertising will therefore be necessary.

Malone feels that in order to show a profit on the SC1 at the earliest possible date, it will be necessary to launch a market campaign to promote it among as wide a range of potential customers, both at home and abroad, as can be covered.

He has therefore called together those people who could normally participate in a market campaign, with a view to working out the outlines, and the costs, of a market campaign, so that if he is asked he has a plan ready to hand. Those called to the meeting are Roger Winfield (Malone's Assistant), Dennis Evans, Charles Spence, Tom Driver, Gerald Durban (Head of Public Relations and Advertising), Tim Howatt (Sales Literature Editor), William Jenkins (Head of the Overseas Sales Department), Henry Wall (Head of Market Research) and Jean Smith (Secretary).

Re-enact this meeting and draft an outline of a market campaign to promote sales of the SC1 both in the U.K. and Europe.

Written follow-up Write up a draft of the market campaign you have decided on.

BEFORE THE BOARD

As Downes had decided not to discuss the SC1 at the last Board meeting. Malone had more time to prepare a full report on the SC1. This report had to be ready for circulation by the 20th August, and Malone started work on it immediately.

When Driver gave him the production figures for the report on the SC1, Malone at first couldn't believe them. Driver maintained that Bellcrest's production capacity would have to be increased by 20% if they were to go ahead with the SC1. Driver gave three reasons for this. Firstly, the fire had affected production, secondly Bellcrest had a lot of new, long-term orders for existing product lines, and thirdly, Orpenshaw had changed the specifications of the SC1 itself, making it a much bigger production job. Malone decided he would have to look into this in detail on the following day.

When Malone finished his report, he submitted it to Downes, who said it was simply not good enough. Malone asked him why he thought this, and Downes replied that he doubted if the Board would agree to back the SC1 on the evidence given in the report. There were the discouraging findings from M.P. Consultants, there were Tom Driver's production figures and there were Malone's own sales forecasts, which Downes felt were far too optimistic. Despite Malone's objections, Downes refused to change his opinion, although he respected Malone's enthusiasm and convictions. Malone asked if he could arrange a demonstration of the SC1 for the Board, and Downes agreed, although he doubted if Malone could arrange one in the two weeks before the Board meeting.

Malone immediately went to see Orpenshaw and asked him whether he could rig up a demonstration of the SC1 for the Board. Orpenshaw told him he was mad, as he should know it was much too early to put the SC1 in a vehicle. Malone insisted. He told Orpenshaw he would give him all the help he could, but that in two weeks the SC1 must be fitted to some sort of vehicle.

Malone then returned to his office, where he had a telephone call from Dr Perkins. Dr Perkins had some very good news from Cremorne Cars for him.

Two weeks later the Board met. Malone was present to explain and defend his report. His proposal to revive the SC1 was greeted with a mixture of surprise and scepticism. Needham pointed out that the SC1 was a new product and that as 80% of all new products failed, he wondered what made the SC1 so much better than other AC speed controls. To this Malone replied that up till then speed controls of this sort had been large and heavy, whereas the SC1 was small, light and could be offered at a low price. Sir Keith Frisby, a member of the Board and an engineer, stated that what he knew of the SC1 led him to believe that Bellcrest had made an important technical breakthrough. Despite Sir Keith's support for the SC1, the Board remained unconvinced. They also wanted to know who actually used an AC speed control and what potential market there was for it. Malone drew their attention to a supplement to his report, in which full details of potential customers were given. When one Board member asked if they could see the SC1 itself, Malone invited them to a demonstration.

The Board were very impressed with the demonstration. Malone disclosed that the small electric car was being developed for city use by Cremorne Cars, who had asked Bellcrest to carry out some tests for them using the SC1 Spence was enthusiastic about the SC1, which was unusual for him, and even Needham was impressed.

When the Board returned to the Boardroom, there was quite a different atmosphere. Downes re-opened the discussion by pointing out that Ashburnham's Bank would only continue the loan if Bellcrest needed it to finance worthwhile development projects. Needham interrupted to say that in his opinion the SC1 was not a worthwhile project, and referred to the required increase of 20% in Bellcrest's production capacity. He also wanted to know where the money would come from to increase Bellcrest's production capacity. One of the Board members suggested that the money could be advanced by Ashburnham's, but Needham stated that he doubted very much whether the Bank would advance money just to launch the SC1. He went on to suggest that it might be better to sub-contract. Downes intervened to point out that sub-contracting would mean that Bellcrest would lose the chance of diversifying successfully, something that the Bank itself insisted on. Downes was supported by the other Board members, and a motion was passed stating that Bellcrest 'should continue development of the SC1 and that the Chairman should look for the necessary capital, starting with the Bank'. Needham refused to support the motion.

After the meeting Downes tried to find out from Needham why he was opposing the SC1. Needham, however, refused to tell him. He merely said he had a train to catch, that he was not in a position to comment and that the final decision was Sir Frederick's, not his. He made the mistake of telling Downes that Bellcrest was not the only firm developing an AC speed control. Downes knew that the only other firm in this field was Electrovans, and realized that Electrovans must be Bellcrest's rival for the Bank's money and that it was from Electrovans that Needham had been getting his information, and not from Janet Malone as Needham had implied at the last Board meeting. Downes was naturally furious at this.

When Malone came to see him, Downes said he owed Janet an apology. Malone was also extremely angry with Needham, and agreed with Downes that he would have to pick up some flowers on his way home! Downes promised Malone that Electrovans would not get the money from the Bank to develop their speed control if he had anything to do with it. Malone now had both the Board's and Downes' support for the SC1.

When Needham returned to the Bank, he saw Sir Frederick Ashburnham. Despite Needham's support for Electrovans, Sir Frederick stated that he had not yet made up his mind which company to support.

EXERCISES

Exercise A **Complete the following sentences:**

1 Sir Keith Frisby was impressed by the r. on the SC1. From the report he j. that Bellcrest had made an important technical b. . Needham interrupted, and Downes insisted that Malone should be allowed to e. his report and d. his recommendations. Another Board member said that the report s. the importance of electric vehicles, although no such market e. as yet.

2 After the demonstration, Needham s. to the Board that the SC1 was not a w. project. He stated that the Bank would not a. the money to launch it, and that the best a. he could give was for Bellcrest to s. -c. to a firm that was better s. to making such products.

3 One of the Board members wished to put a m. to the e. that the company should continue development of the SC1. He also suggested that the Chairman should look for the necessary c. The m. was duly s. and p. by a large majority. Needham did not s. the m. , although he was the only one to o. it.

Exercise B *Downes and Malone discussed the SC1 last week.*
Write a report of their conversation using these verbs:

For Downes: suggest, feel, enquire, believe, maintain, add, ask, wonder.
For Malone: insist, regret, disclose, complain, explain, deny, admit, assure.

Downes: Well, Paul, it's my belief that the SC1 is finished.
Malone: Really, I must protest. You're not giving me the support I need.
Downes: A question, Paul. Why is the SC1 going to be such a big production job?
Malone: There's a simple explanation. Orpenshaw has changed the specifications.
Downes: I see. And another thing: the report is taking a long time.
Malone: I have to tell you I haven't finished it.
Downes: Your wife has been rather indiscreet, hasn't she?
Malone: No, not at all. She doesn't give away company secrets.
Downes: Well, what about the consultants? Are they any good, I wonder?
Malone: Oh, don't worry. They're a very sound firm.
Downes: I have a feeling rumours really aren't enough, you know.
Malone: I'm sorry I can't get anything in writing.
Downes: And why must you make such a secret of the demonstration?
Malone: Well, I think I can tell you that Cremorne Cars have agreed to let us carry out tests with their car.
Downes: I still say there may not be any car for all we know.
Malone: Look, I'm certain about this, I tell you. Cremorne Cars are intending to develop a commuter car.

Exercise C **Complete the following sentences:**

Example:
Have you ever been to Majorca?
He asked if I had ever been to Majorca.

1 Have you seen Needham recently?
He asked

2 Is there any chance of reviving the SC1?
He wondered

3 Do you know what time the meeting is?
He asked

4 I don't understand why the Bank is withdrawing the loan.
He didn't know

5 Tell me how the SC1 works.
Spence wanted to know

6 I have my doubts about the suitability of the SC1
Needham doubted suitable.

7 Will the report be ready soon?
He asked

8 I'd like to know who takes the minutes.
He wanted to find out

9 Did we decide to sell the SC1? I can't remember.
He couldn't remember

10 Does the meeting begin at two or half past two?
He wasn't sure half past two.

Exercise D **Complete these sentences using 'could have' or 'was able to':**

Malone's first problem was production. If he had wanted to, Driver (insist) on the impossibility of producing the SC1, but Malone (persuade) him that production capacity could be increased sufficiently. Due to postponement of the discussion until the next Board meeting, Malone (spend) more time on the report but in spite of his efforts he (not convince) Downes. The Managing Director (abandon) the SC1 at this point, but Malone (get) permission to arrange a demonstration for the Board. Bad news from M.P. Consultants (also endanger) the project but fortunately Dr Perkins (produce) some encouraging figures. All this meant that Malone (put forward) a good case for the SC1. The Board agreed to support the project, although they (so easily reject) it.

Exercise E **Written Task**

At the demonstration, Sir Keith Frisby was very impressed by the performance of the SC1. As an engineer he wanted to find out as much as he could about it, so he wrote to Malone. Write this letter for him.

to congratulate you
most impressed
would like to know more
assure you of my support.

DRILLS

Drill 1 *Bellcrest has treated the SC1 as highly confidential, but it is very difficult to keep things secret in the motor industry. There have been a great many rumours. So many, in fact, that Bellcrest's competitors don't know what to believe.*

I've heard that Bellcrest have decided to expand.
ARE YOU SURE OF THAT? WHEN I LAST SPOKE TO DOWNES HE TOLD ME THAT THE RANGE OF PRODUCTS HAD BEEN REDUCED.

I believe they have spent a lot on development.
ARE YOU SURE OF THAT? WHEN I LAST SPOKE TO ORPENSHAW HE COMPLAINED THAT R. AND D. PROJECTS HAD BEEN AXED.

1 Downes/told/range of products/reduce
2 Orpenshaw/complained/R. and D. projects/axe
3 Malone/said/the project/abandon
4 Needham/told/the patents/sell

5 Driver/insisted/the offer/reject
6 Urwin/denied/a contract/sign
7 Needham/admitted/Bellcrest's proposals/consider
8 Spence/insisted/the question/not discuss

Drill 2 *The Directors of Bellcrest went to the R. and D. area to watch a demonstration of the SC1. This demonstration was also watched by Bill and Harry, two of the cleaners at the factory. They knew nothing about the SC1, and had no idea what was going on. They were interested but didn't understand what they had seen, and afterwards they had this conversation.*

Bill, who were these men?
I'VE NO IDEA WHO THEY WERE.

Bill, does that car run on batteries?
I'VE NO IDEA WHAT IT RUNS ON.

Drill 3 Did Orpenshaw make the SC1 smaller?
YES, FORTUNATELY HE WAS ABLE TO MAKE THE SC1 SMALLER.

Did he insist on having more time?
WELL, HE COULD HAVE INSISTED ON HAVING MORE TIME, BUT HE DIDN'T.

1 yes	3 well	5 yes	7 yes
2 well	4 yes	6 well	8 well

Dialogue **Showing a product to a visitor**
Paul Malone is showing one of Bellcrest's products to a visitor.

I SHOULD BE VERY HAPPY TO GIVE YOU
I'd be glad

ANY FURTHER INFORMATION YOU MAY NEED ON IT.
details require.

IF I MAY REFER YOU TO PAGE EIGHT OF THE BROCHURE,
If I may draw your attention to leaflet,
If you'd like to look at

YOU'LL FIND ALL THE SPECIFICATIONS THERE.

OUR TESTS INDICATE THAT THIS MODEL HAS A SERVICE LIFE OF
show minimum service life of
AT LEAST 55,000 HOURS.

OH, NO, FAR FROM IT. THAT'S ABOUT 5,000 HOURS LONGER
Oh, no, not at all. approximately
Oh, no, certainly not.

THAN ANY OTHER MAKE IN ITS PRICE RANGE.
all other makes at that price.

IF THAT WERE TO HAPPEN, JUST CONTACT
If that did happen. you only have to get in touch with

OUR NEAREST AGENT AND HE'LL SEND SOMEONE ROUND
a man

IMMEDIATELY.
at once.
the same day.

YES, WE DO INDEED. OUR USUAL FIGURE IS AROUND 5%,
Certainly we do. normal about

BUT THAT DEPENDS ON THE SIZE OF THE ORDER.
how large the order is.

NOT AT ALL. I HOPE WE SHALL BE HEARING FROM YOU
trust hear

VERY SHORTLY.
soon.

Drill 4 *A telephone call has just been put through to Paul Malone's office.*

Yes.
Oh, yes . . .
That's right.
Mmm . . . . .
Mm-hm . . .
That's marvellous!
Oh dear!
I'm afraid so.
No . . .
No.
That's marvellous!
No, that's all right.
Fine.
Thank you very much, Mr. Veazy.

Drill 5 *Malone is very pleased with the car supplied by Cremorne Cars for the demonstration of the SC1. After the demonstration, he sends a telegram to Cremorne Cars. He dictates the telegram letter by letter to the telephonist.*

K. VEAZY. CREMORNE CARS SLOUGH. CONGRATULATIONS. YOUR W. J. PROTOTYPE IDEAL OUR PURPOSES. DEMONSTRATION UNQUALIFIED SUCCESS. MALONE.

ACTIVE LISTENING

Malone is ringing up Alan Beeston to offer him the post of Product Executive.

1 Why does Malone offer to wait a week for his decision?

. . . .

. . . .

2 What does Beeston want to know about his salary?

. . . .

. . . .

3 How much better off will he be in his new job?

. . . .

. . . .

4 Who are Beeston's present employers and when will he stop working for them?

. . . .

. . . .

5 Why does Malone want Beeston to start work quickly, do you think, and why can't Beeston do so?

. . . .

. . . .

6 What does Beeston want Bellcrest to help him do?

. . . .

. . . .

7 What help will Bellcrest provide?

. . . .

. . . .

8 Why will Beeston visit Bellcrest the following week?

. . . .

. . . .

9 What must he bring with him?

. . . .

. . . .

10 Why does Malone want to know Beeston's bank account number?

. . . .

. . . .

11 What does Beeston want Malone to do, and why?

. . . .

. . . .

ROLE SIMULATION

Statement of Problem In this episode the Bellcrest Board discussed Malone's report and came to a decision on whether or not to support the SC1.

You should now re-enact this Board meeting. It is not necessary for you to come to the same decision as the Board did. Use your own judgement. Malone, the Marketing Manager, has submitted his report to you, and you are free to ask him any further questions you like before coming to a decision. The demonstration has already taken place.

Written follow-up Write a summary of your discussion and the decision you reached.

APPOINTMENTS

Downes now had the approval of his Board to go ahead with the SC1 provided that Bellcrest could raise the necessary capital. He had also learned that Electrovans were competing for the Bank's money to develop their own AC speed control, and that Needham at least was backing them, so the obvious source for the money Bellcrest needed was very uncertain. Downes decided to ring up Sir Frederick so as to arrange a meeting.

Sir Frederick was pleased to have some definite information about Bellcrest's plans so that he could assess their claim to the Bank's money. Sir Frederick had already discussed Bellcrest's last Board meeting with Needham, from which he understood that Bellcrest wanted the money so as to finance the launching of the SC1. Downes asked for a meeting so that he could explain how the SC1 would benefit the Bank, and added that he did not feel Bellcrest was being fairly represented by Needham. Sir Frederick agreed to a discussion, but said he would not be free until the following week.

Soon after Downes had finished speaking to Sir Frederick, he had a telephone call from Sam Urwin in Toronto. Urwin wanted to meet Downes to discuss something that he described as being personal and urgent. Downes would have preferred to meet Urwin after talking to Sir Frederick the following Wednesday, but Urwin insisted on meeting him before then as he was visiting Electrovans on Wednesday and he had to make an important decision before seeing Williams. Downes agreed to see him the following Tuesday.

Urwin arrived the following Tuesday. As he was walking to Bellcrest he was almost run over by one of the Cremorne electric cars. Downes, who was watching from his window, was amused by this, but felt he had better get Driver to issue a memo to all drivers telling them to be more careful in future.

When Urwin arrived in Downes' office he said he wanted to talk about Donald Williams and Electrovans in the strictest confidence. He asked for Downes' advice on whether he could trust Williams, and showed Downes a brochure that Electrovans had recently distributed in North America which implied that his corporation was already an Electrovans customer, which was not in fact the case. Urwin said it was true that he was negotiating

with Williams, and that negotiations had reached the stage where he had to say 'yes' or 'no'. He added that although a contract had been drafted it had not yet been signed. Urwin had looked at Electrovans' company records and said they looked all right, but he still wasn't entirely happy. Downes said that in his opinion Urwin would be safe if he signed the contract.

Downes then had a number of questions he wanted to ask Urwin. He wanted to know why Urwin had been talking to him as if he was no more than an old friend, when Bellcrest already had an agreement with Passlee Electronics. Urwin pointed out that this was a non-exclusive agreement, but Downes refused to accept this as an excuse. He accused Urwin of going behind his back, as Urwin must have known from Electrovans' sales literature that they were moving into Bellcrest's field. Urwin defended himself by saying that what he wanted was outside Bellcrest's field – an AC speed control for electric vehicles. Downes reminded Urwin of the car that had nearly run him over earlier and told him it was fitted with a Bellcrest AC speed control.

Urwin was extremely annoyed that he hadn't been told earlier that Bellcrest was developing an AC speed control. He said that if he had been kept in the picture there would have been no trouble with Electrovans, as if he had known what Bellcrest was doing he would never have gone to Electrovans at all. He said that this time Downes would regret his usual caution, but he agreed to have a look at the SC1.

After he had obtained the approval of the Board for the SC1, Malone got in touch with Alan Beeston and offered him a job as a product executive, which he accepted. When he came to Bellcrest, Malone told him he hoped he would be responsible for the SC1, though this was not yet definite. To Malone's surprise, Beeston already knew that Electrovans was developing a speed control and he had in fact turned down a job with them. He went on to say that Electrovans' future didn't look too bright, so he was glad he had not accepted it. He then revealed that Beamish Motors, who accounted for over 40% of all Electrovans' business, had stopped doing business with them and that all orders had been switched to other suppliers. Malone was astonished and hurried off to tell Downes the news.

Malone found Downes with Orpenshaw and Urwin in the Research and Development Area, where they were looking at the SC1. Orpenshaw was just telling Urwin that Electrovans was more than five years behind Bellcrest in the development of its speed control, so he was wasting his time buying from them. Urwin was clearly annoyed and obviously had plenty to say about the SC1, but said he would prefer to say it in Downes' office. Downes and Urwin then left, so Malone was unable to tell Downes the vital piece of information that Beeston had brought.

After Downes and Urwin had left, Orpenshaw said he was surprised that nobody had told Urwin about the SC1. Malone agreed that this time Downes' caution had lost the biggest customer they were likely to get.

EXERCISES

Exercise A **Complete the following sentences:**

1 At the Board meeting Downes won the a. of his Board to g. a. with the SC1 provided that he could r. the money to l. it. Ashburnham's Bank, the obvious s. of this money, seemed to be b. Electrovans so Downes rang Sir Frederick to arrange a meeting to discuss the whole matter.

2 Sir Frederick was glad to have the information on the SC1, as he could then a. Bellcrest's c. to the Bank's money. Downes told Sir Frederick he could argue Bellcrest's c. in detail against any r. the Bank could p. u.

3 Sir Frederick told his secretary to a. an a. with Downes for the following week. His secretary wanted to know what time would s. Downes, who told her that three o'clock on Wednesday would be c.

Exercise B **Complete the following sentences:**

Urwin: Maurice, I almost got run down in the yard just now. I was walking over to the main office when this damn little car nearly took the pants off me. If he (blow) his horn, I (hear) him and gotten out of the way.

Downes: My apologies, Sam. But if you (look) where you were going, you (see) him, I expect.

Urwin: Well, if your drivers (race) around like that every day as they seem to be doing, you (soon have) some

	accidents. Maybe if you (tell) them to be careful, do you think they (drive) a little slower?
Downes:	Yes, if we (tell) our drivers to drive slowly, then they (do) it.
Urwin:	If you (can) do that, I (be) grateful.
Downes:	We don't have accidents here, you know.
Urwin:	If you (do have) an accident, it (really wake you up) wouldn't it?
Downes:	O.K. I (ask) Driver to see to it if you (think) it's necessary.
Urwin:	Thanks. Then if I (go out) again, maybe I (not get) run over. And if you (do) that before, I (not be) in danger in the first place.

Exercise C When Malone writes down notes in his diary he often uses signs instead of words so as to save time.

For example he uses the sign → to show either *the reason for* or *the result of* an action.

Example:
Give Downes the facts → he can present his report.
I'll have to give Downes the facts so that he can present his report.

Here are some notes from Malone's diary.
Make complete sentences using: 'so/so that/so as to'.

1 Present a strong case → be able to convince the Board.
2 Get hold of car → have to negotiate with Cremorne Cars.
3 Orpenshaw arrange demonstration → Board will see the advantages.
4 Brief Beeston → Jean will have to make an appointment for next week.
5 Must see Urwin → must find out which hotel he's in.
6 Forget to give Driver report → figures have not been checked.
7 Write to Mandl → answer his questions.
8 Jean off sick → Betty must type letters.
9 Take car into garage → engine can be repaired.
10 Downes says Janet indiscreet → must ask her about Needham.

Exercise D *You have received the following telegrams.*
Write out the messages in complete sentences.

1 SEND SIX HUNDRED OFF FIVE TWO SEVENS STOP
2 MEET REP ARRIVING PANAM FOUR THREE ONE WEDNESDAY STOP
3 PRESIDENT PASSLEE QUOTE DEAL OFF UNQUOTE STOP ARRANGE MEETING STOP

4 NEED SURGE DIVERTERS URGENT STOP ORDER FIVE HUNDRED STOP
5 ORDER EIGHTH INST UNARRIVED STOP ATTEND URGENT STOP

Exercise E **Written Task**

Malone has to write to Beeston confirming an offer he made by telephone. You write this letter for him. Use these notes:

Offer you post of Product Executive
Start September 14th
Salary £2,500
4 weeks holiday
Duties
Assistance with accommodation
Please confirm acceptance
Send insurance card, bank account number

DRILLS

Drill 1 Bellcrest wants to diversify.
THEY WOULD DIVERSIFY IF THEY LAUNCHED A NEW PRODUCT.

1 launch/new product
2 Bank/approve/project
3 facts/figures/ready
4 know/project
5 demonstrate/SC1

Williams left Bellcrest
HE WOULDN'T HAVE LEFT IF DOWNES HADN'T GIVEN HIM THE SACK.

6 Downes/give/sack
7 Williams/copy/design
8 Bank/threaten/withdraw loan
9 Downes/keep/in the dark
10 Malone/warn

Drill 2 Why did Bellcrest have to ask for a loan?
THEY HAD TO ASK FOR A LOAN SO AS TO FINANCE NEW PROJECTS.

And why were all those new projects launched?
THEY WERE LAUNCHED SO THAT LONG-TERM PROFITS COULD BE INCREASED.

1 finance new projects
2 long-term profits/can/be increased
3 capture a growing market
4 meeting/can/arrange
5 obtain the facts
6 Bank/can/assess/Bellcrest's claim
7 financial questions/can/settle
8 avoid/see/Needham

Dialogue **Arranging a meeting**

Sam Urwin telephones Downes to arrange a meeting for the following week.

SAM! WHERE ARE YOU SPEAKING FROM?
phoning
calling

TOWARDS THE END OF THE WEEK WOULD SUIT ME BEST.
be best for me.
be most convenient for me.

I'LL BE IN LONDON ON WEDNESDAY. WOULD THAT BE ANY USE TO YOU
Would that help you at all?

SORRY, SAM. THIS LINE'S BAD. WOULD YOU MIND REPEATING THA
awful. Would you say that again?
terrible.

WOULD TUESDAY AFTERNOON BE ALL RIGHT?
suit you?

I CAN'T MANAGE THE MORNING.
I can't make the morning.
I'm tied up in the morning.

YES, OF COURSE, SAM, WHAT'S ALL THE HURRY ABOUT?
why the hurry?

I SEE. WELL, I LOOK FORWARD TO SEEING
Ah ha. meeting
YOU ON TUESDAY AFTERNOON. TWO THIRTY'D BE FINE.
quite all right.

BYE, SAM.
Cheerio, Sam.

Drill 3 *Alan Beeston is in Paul Malone's office. They are discussing Beeston's new job. Beeston has a number of things for which he wants to ask Malone's permission.*

I'm hoping Bellcrest will pay my removal expenses. I don't think it'll be very much.
I'M SURE THAT'LL BE ALL RIGHT, AS LONG AS IT ISN'T TOO MUCH.

Drill 4 *Beeston and Malone are still talking. Malone is telling Beeston about his work at Bellcrest. Beeston has a number of questions he wants to ask.*

Now, you'll be doing several kinds of work.
BEFORE WE GO ANY FURTHER, I'D LIKE TO KNOW SOMETHING MORE ABOUT THE KINDS OF WORK I'LL BE DOING.

ACTIVE LISTENING

Malone thinks that the AC speed control developed by Electrovans will infringe Bellcrest's patents. He decided to consult Mr Howard, a specialist in patent law.

1 Who suggested that Malone should consult Howard?

2 What does Malone do first before discussing his problem with Howard?

3 When he has heard this, what is the first thing Howard wants to know?

4 What has led Malone to suspect that there has been an infringement of patents?

5 What did Orpenshaw think he would have to do if he joined the other firm?

6 Why does Howard advise Malone to get more information?

7 At what point does an infringement of patent occur?

8 Why is it difficult for Malone to confirm his suspicions?

9 In what way is British patent law different from that of many other European countries?

10 Could Malone go to a law court at this stage?

11 What does Howard warn Malone about?

12 What does he advise him to do?

ROLE SIMULATION

Statement of Problem

Alan Beeston will be taking up his appointment at the beginning of next week. During his first week with Bellcrest he will need to be introduced to the work of a number of departments. It has therefore been suggested that he should meet the Heads of the Departments with whom he will have to co-operate. Malone's secretary, Jean Smith, has tried to draw up a timetable for Beeston's first week, but unfortunately everybody's diaries are rather full.

Beeston himself wants to visit the various departments in a particular order. As Malone wants the timetable settled as quickly as possible, he has asked all those concerned to drop into his office at 5.30, after work, to be introduced to Beeston and arrange a time when he can call on them the following week.

The object of this short meeting is therefore to arrange a timetable for Beeston without interfering with anyone's existing arrangements.

Written follow-up

Imagine you are Jean Smith. Draw up a timetable for Beeston as decided on at your meeting, stating the purpose of each meeting that has been arranged.

AGREEMENT.

Malone was unable to give Downes Beeston's information about Electrovans losing their largest customer when Downes and Urwin were in the Research and Development area, so he followed them to Downes' office. Although Downes tried to stop him, Malone insisted on attacking Urwin's decision to make a deal with Electrovans. He forced Urwin to admit that the SC1 was better than Electrovans' speed control, but Urwin immediately pointed out that Electrovans were tooled up to produce their speed control and that Williams had already given him a firm delivery date for the first units. Malone then revealed that Electrovans had just lost their biggest customer.

Downes and Urwin reacted to this news in different ways. Downes was surprised and suggested that Electrovans might be in real trouble, whereas Urwin felt this would help him as Electrovans would be freer to concentrate on producing their speed control. Malone jumped on this and said it might well not be Electrovans' speed control at all, as he was pretty sure that their design infringed the Bellcrest patents. If that was the case, he added, Bellcrest would certainly take out an injunction ordering Electrovans to stop production.

Urwin was by now very angry, as he felt that Malone and Downes were being obstructive. He said he might well cancel his agreements with Bellcrest if Bellcrest took out an injunction against Electrovans to stop production of the speed controls he urgently needed. Downes said if Urwin signed a contract with Electrovans, he would terminate the agreement himself. He went on to say that naturally he didn't expect Urwin to make a decision on trust, and Malone added that he would give Urwin all the data he needed on the SC1. Finally Urwin agreed to tell his Technical Manager to join him at Bellcrest that day rather than the following day at Electrovans, but that was as far as he would go. Urwin's decision was vital to Bellcrest.

The following day Downes went to the Bank to argue his case for the SC1, and to keep hold of the Bank's investment in Bellcrest. Before he arrived, Needham argued in favour of giving the loan to Electrovans, as he felt that they were more qualified to produce an AC speed control. Sir Frederick insisted, however, on allowing Downes to argue his case. At that moment Downes arrived with a visitor Needham was unable to identify.

Downes started his argument for the Bank's loan staying with Bellcrest by telling Sir Frederick that Electrovans had just lost all their orders from Beamish Motors, which amounted to 45% in volume of business. Needham said that this might well mean that Electrovans could concentrate on producing their speed control, and added that they already had one large and urgent order from North America. Downes then sprang a surprise on Sir Frederick and Needham by telling them that this was Passlee Electronics, and that Passlee's Executive Vice-President, Sam Urwin, was waiting outside. He asked Sir Frederick if he might invite Urwin to join them and Sir Frederick agreed, although he thought it highly irregular.

When Urwin had been introduced, he announced that he was calling off his deal with Electrovans, as the Electrovans' design appeared to infringe the Bellcrest patents. Needham said that Williams had assured him there was no infringement of the Bellcrest patents, but on Sir Frederick's asking whether the information had been checked, he had to admit that it hadn't. Needham went on to say that in any case he could see a solution to the problem, but Downes immediately interrupted him to say that Bellcrest were not going to sell the patents. Sir Frederick then asked Downes for his solution. Downes said that the Bank loan could stay with Bellcrest as the money would certainly be needed to finish development and start production of the SC1. Sir Frederick wondered how Bellcrest was going to meet orders that were needed quickly, such as Urwin's, and how and where the SC1 was actually going to be produced. Downes said that Bellcrest could sub-contract. Sir Frederick thanked him for this suggestion and announced that the loan would stay with Bellcrest, provided that Electrovans was the sub-contractor. Downes protested that he would not sit at the same table with Williams, but Sir Frederick ignored this and instructed Needham to arrange a meeting. Needham tried to prevent this, but Sir Frederick firmly said he would talk to him later.

The meeting between Downes and Williams was arranged to take place in a quiet hotel where there would be no publicity. Downes, Spence and Malone arrived first. Downes was surprised to find Joy Banks there, the journalist who had interviewed him at the time of the Bellcrest fire. When Williams arrived, he was sarcastic about Malone's presence, and told Downes that talking about the SC1 reminded him of his time at Bellcrest. He then insisted that Downes should shake hands with him, and as they did so, Joy Banks took a photograph, which appeared next day in the Midland News.

Downes was furious at this trick, and went to the Bank the following day. He asked Sir Frederick whether he realized that Williams had arranged for the photograph to be taken, and pointed out that no-one could conduct business with a man who behaved like that. Sir Frederick agreed that the incident was most unfortunate, but maintained that Electrovans were the ideal firm to make the SC1. Downes didn't deny this, but said that Williams had to go, otherwise he could not agree to Electrovans being the sub-contractor. Sir Frederick said that the Bank did not sack Managing Directors, but when Downes replied that Bellcrest should be represented on the Electrovans Board, he said the Bank would welcome such a link. Downes was immediately worried that this representative would be Needham, but Sir Frederick assured him it wouldn't. He added that Needham would be replaced as the Bank's representative on the Bellcrest Board. Sir Frederick then mentioned that Williams had been offered another job, which meant that the post of Managing Director of Electrovans would be vacant for someone Downes could trust as he was sure Williams would be wise enough to accept the job he had been offered.

Later that day Downes called on Malone and told him that he would be appointed Managing Director of Electrovans.

EXERCISES

Exercise A **Complete the following sentences:**

1 Downes was unwilling to co-operate with Williams mainly because he had no t. in him. He was unable to t. a man who had clearly been less then h. in his dealings with Passlee Electronics. The events of five years previously had already destroyed any g. that might have existed between the two men and left an atmosphere of m. Downes h. no c. in the h. of Williams, so when he announced that Electrovans' speed control did not infringe Bellcrest patents, Downes certainly did not t. this on t. and began to make enquiries about the matter. His lack of confidence in their honesty was in the end well j. , and Downes was glad he had p. his t. in his own judgement.

2 Downes was anxious that Electrovans should be m. with Bellcrest rather than becoming a c. in the same field. Sir Frederick Ashburnham, however, was against a m. and preferred Electrovans to manufacture the speed control units as s. – c. to Bellcrest. Downes opposed any such arrangement and continued to put the case for a t. o. . He finally agreed to Sir Frederick's proposals on condition that Bellcrest should be r. on the Board of Electrovans by a completely t. person.

Exercise B **Rewrite the following sentences using 'can' or 'may':**

Examples:
It's possible Williams will join Beamish Motors.
Williams may join Beamish Motors.

At last we have enough time to visit customers.
At last we can visit customers.

1 Joy Banks has a good story to write about Downes and Williams.
2 Malone will probably reorganize Electrovans.
3 He's in a position to realize all his plans.
4 The Malones are thinking about moving house.
5 Orpenshaw has the time to concentrate on his technical work now.
6 Now the Malones have enough money to buy a new car.
7 The immediate appointment of a new marketing manager is likely.
8 Downes feels able to speak to Electrovans' Managing Director now.
9 Beamish Motors will perhaps buy from Electrovans again.
10 The R. and D. section will probably be rehoused.

Exercise C *Downes, Urwin and Malone are having an argument about Urwin's deal with Electrovans.*

Complete the sentences:

Downes: If you buy from Electrovans, Sam, our agreement with Passlee may (terminate)

Urwin: Now, don't blame me for going to Electrovans. It's your own fault, Maurice. I should (tell) about the SC1 long ago.

Downes: But surely you see that it was necessary to keep it a secret? If our competitors had found out, it would (be) bad for business.

Urwin: Keeping quiet about it has been even worse for business. This deal with Electrovans might never (consider) if you had trusted me with your secret. As it is I cannot (expect) to reverse my decision now.

Malone: But, Sam, the SC1 is so much better than anything that could (design) by Electrovans.

Urwin: The Electrovans design may not (be) better than the SC1, but at least they have the resources to put it on the market. You can't deny, Paul, that the SC1 cannot (produce) without difficulty. And I just do not believe that their design infringes your patents. That must (check) before they went ahead.

Malone: You don't know Williams. Anyway, Electrovans has just lost its biggest customer. Their ability to produce could (affect) by this.

Urwin: If I had had this information earlier, I might (prepare) to cancel negotiations. But it is too late now. The contract should (sign) the day after tomorrow.

Exercise D **Complete the sentences using 'despite the fact that' and 'whereas':**

1 Urwin was negotiating a deal with Electrovans he still had an agreement with Bellcrest.
2 Williams knew about the SC1 Urwin hadn't been told.
3 Urwin wanted to buy the Electrovans speed control Bellcrest could produce a better one.
4 Downes was pessimistic about Bellcrest's chances Malone was rather more hopeful.
5 Electrovans was going ahead with its speed control it probably infringed Bellcrest patents.
6 Bellcrest intended to produce the SC1 it was right outside their normal field.
7 Electrovans was ready to produce a speed control Bellcrest had only just decided to revive their project.
8 Bellcrest was in a strong position Electrovans had just lost its biggest customer.
9 Downes is a sound man Williams is very adventurous.
10 Downes agreed to launch the new project he is usually very cautious.

Exercise E **Written Task**

Write Sir Frederick's letter to Downes confirming the extension of the loan, arrangements for production of the SC1 and management changes at Electrovans.

DRILLS

Drill 1 Is it possible that the Electrovans design infringes our patents?
YES, IT MAY INFRINGE OUR PATENTS.

If this is the case, have we the right to take legal action?
YES, WE CAN TAKE LEGAL ACTION.

Drill 2 *It is quarter to eleven and Beeston hasn't yet arrived at Bellcrest where he has an appointment for ten o'clock. Malone asks Jean about this.*

Wasn't Beeston's train due some time ago?
MM. IT SHOULD HAVE BEEN IN AN HOUR AGO.

We can expect him any time now.
MM. HE SHOULD BE HERE ANY TIME NOW.

1 should/in/an hour ago
2 should/here/any time now
3 may/coming/car
4 may/caught/rush hour
5 could/delayed/by the fog
6 might not/here/before twelve
7 must/on his way then
8 should/informed/delay
9 must/prevented/getting here
10 could/in an accident

Dialogue **Dealing with a complaint**

Paul Malone is in his office when a customer rings him up.

MALONE.
Malone here.

SPEAKING.
Yes, that's right.

I'M SORRY TO HEAR THAT, MR BURTON.
you say so,

NATURALLY NOT, MR BURTON. COULD YOU GIVE ME THE INVOICE
Of course not, NUMBER?

RIGHT, I'VE GOT THAT. I'LL LOOK INTO IT IMMEDIATELY, MR BURTON.
I see. I'll make enquiries immediately,

I'LL FIND OUT WHAT'S HAPPENED AND RING YOU BACK WITHIN HALF
I'll see phone AN HOUR.
call

OF COURSE. I'M VERY SORRY THERE'S BEEN A DELAY.
Naturally. about this delay.
I must apologize for this delay.

YOU'LL CERTAINLY HAVE THEM BY THEN, MR BURTON.
definitely receive

YES, OF COURSE.
Yes, certainly.

GOODBYE, MR BURTON.

Drill 3 *Maurice Downes and Sam Urwin are arguing about the SC1. Downes is trying to persuade Urwin to change his mind about buying from Electrovans, but Urwin is being very firm.*

I know you came to England with plans to buy the speed control, but isn't it possible to put off your decision?
LOOK HERE MAURICE, I'VE MADE UP MY MIND TO BUY THE SPEED CONTROL. I DON'T INTEND TO PUT OFF MY DECISION WITHOUT A GOOD REASON.

Drill 4 *Paul Malone has just taken up his new job as Managing Director of Electrovans. He is talking to his Marketing Manager, George Turpin. They are planning the production and marketing of the SC1.*

1 Get ready for production: complete tests/equip a production line.
2 Produce SC1: increase production capacity/find more capital.
3 Increase production capacity: work overtime/take on new staff.
4 Take on new staff: select them carefully/train them.
5 Launch the SC1: prepare brochures/plan publicity campaign.
6 Sell the SC1: find customers/appoint agents.
7 Export the SC1: appoint overseas agents/learn foreign languages.
8 Learn a foreign language: attend a course/work hard.

ACTIVE LISTENING

Malone makes the acquaintance of Mr MacLeod, the Managing Director of a subsidiary company, and invites him home to discuss the problems of subsidiaries. Their wives can be heard talking in the background.

1 Has Mr MacLeod's company always been a subsidiary?

. . . .

. . . .

2 Why did the parent company take over a number of smaller firms?

. . . .

. . . .

3 What types of companies were taken over?

. . . .

. . . .

4 Why was Mr MacLeod's company included in the group?

. . . .

. . . .

5 What differences are there between being the Managing Director of an independent company and the Managing Director of a subsidiary?

. . . .

. . . .

6 Are there any disadvantages in being the Managing Director of a subsidiary?

. . . .

. . . .

7 What does the parent company try to persuade subsidiaries to do?

. . . .

. . . .

8 What directorships does Mr MacLeod hold?

. . . .

. . . .

9 What does he mean when he says there is a 'conflict of loyalty' in this set-up?

. . . .

. . . .

10 Why is this combine not typical of British combines?

. . . .

. . . .

11 In what way is this subsidiary company in a special position within the group?

. . . .

. . . .

12 What effect has this had on the parent group?

. . . .

ROLE SIMULATION

Statement of Problem Sir Frederick has decided to call a meeting at which all parties concerned with the Bank's loan are to represented. The purpose of the meeting is to decide whether the Bank's money is to be invested in Bellcrest or Electrovans, or whether a compromise solution should be found. A number of suggestions for a compromise have been made. They include the suggestion that there should be a merger between the two companies, that Bellcrest should sub-contract to Electrovans, and that Bellcrest should sell the SC1 patents to Electrovans and give up this particular field of activity.

Re-enact this meeting and come to your own solution. It is not necessary that you should come to the same solution as Sir Frederick did in the film. What is your solution?

Written follow-up Write a summary of the agreement you have reached.

GLOSSARY

The purpose of the glossary is to help the learner in his reading of the summary, exercises and role-play. Care has been taken to include words which the learner is likely to meet when no recourse to a teacher is possible, e.g. when working at home. Excluded from the glossary are elementary words which the learner is expected to know, e g. 'employ', 'profit', 'possible', obvious derivatives of known elementary words, e.g. 'employee', 'profitable', 'possibly', words of international currency, e.g. 'deal', 'market', 'computer', and words which occur only in the film. Definitions are restricted to the meanings occurring in the course, e.g. 'back' is defined in the context of 'back a project'. The phonetic transcription used is that of the *English Pronouncing Dictionary* by D. Jones. Alternative pronunciations are not given. The glossary is an aid to the learner but not a dictionary. It should be supplemented where necessary by the use of a good dictionary such as *The Advanced Learner's Dictionary of Current English* by A.S. Hornby, E.V. Gatenby and H. Wakefield.

List of Abbreviations

adj.	adjective	n.	noun
adv.	adverb	prep.	preposition
Am.	American	sb.	somebody
conj.	conjunction	sth.	something
e.g.	for example	v.	verb

abandon [əˈbændən] v. abandon the plan = give up the plan

A.C. [ei siː] n. alternating current, flow of electricity in which the positive and negative poles interchange, usually 50 times per second (50 cycles per second) see D.C.

access [ˈækses] n. have access to information = be able to use information

accordance [əˈkɔːdəns] n. in accordance with your instructions = according to your instructions

account [əˈkaunt] n. a bill to be paid; of a firm = accounts department, financial department (see Bellcrest structure plan; bank account = arrangement with a bank to put in and take out money

account [əˈkaunt] n. take into account = take into consideration

account for [əˈkaunt fɔː] v. be the reason for, take up; Beamish Motors account for 50% of Electrovans' business.

accurate [ˈækjurit] adj. exact; accuracy n.

accuse [əˈkjuːz] v. he accused me of lying = he said I had lied; -ation [ˈækjuˈzeiʃən] n.

achieve [əˈtʃiːv] v. do sth. successfully; -ment n.

adapt [əˈdæpt] v. change sth. so that it is more suitable; -ation n.

adequate [ˈædikwit] adj. enough

adjuster [əˈdʒʌstə] n. an insurance adjuster = an official of an insurance company who decides the cost of damage

administer	[əd'ministə] v. manage; administration [əd'mini'streiʃən] n.
advance	[əd'vɑːns] v. advance money = lend money
affect	[ə'fekt] v. have an effect on
agenda	[ə'dʒendə] n. list of matters to be discussed at a meeting
agent	['eidʒənt] n. a person who acts for a business; agency n.
air terminal	['ɛə 'təːminl] n. office and bus station for air-passengers; place in town centre where airport buses arrive and depart
allocate	['æləkeit] v. allocate money to/for sth. = allow so much money for a certain purpose
alternative	[ɔːl'təːnətiv] adj. n. a second possibility
announce	[ə'nauns] v. declare; -ment n.
annoy	[ə'nɔi] v. make sb. angry
annual	['ænjuəl] adj. once a year
anticipate	[æn'tisipeit] v. think of sth. before it happens
apologize	[ə'pɔlədʒaiz] v. say you are sorry; apology [ə'pɔlədʒi] n.
apparent	[ə'pærənt] adj. clear
arise	[ə'raiz] v. a complication has arisen = we have just discovered a complication
assess	[ə'ses] v. decide the value of; -ment n.
assume	[ə'sjuːm] v. believe without evidence/facts
assure	[ə'ʃuə] v. say with certainty; I assure you the money will be paid
atmosphere	['ætməsfiə] n. there was an atmosphere of uncertainty = people felt uncertain
attractive	[ə'træktiv] adj. an attractive offer = an advantageous offer
authority	[ɔː'θɔriti] n. airport authority = those in control of the airport
automotive	['ɔːtəu'məutiv]adj. concerned with self-powered vehicles, particularly private cars; the automotive field
available	[ə'veiləbl] adj. money is available = there is money which can be used
aware	[ə'wɛə] adj. be aware of = realize, know
awkward	['ɔːkwəd] adj. causing difficulties
axe	[æks] v. the project was axed = the project was discontinued
back	[bæk] v. support
basis	['beisis] n. starting-point; base [beis] v.
battery	[bætəri] n. object containing metal plates and chemicals for making electricity
benefit	['benifit] v. n. help
Board of Directors	['bɔːd əv di'rektəz] n. group of men controlling a company, elected by and representing the shareholders
bound to	['baund tu] adj. production is bound to suffer = production will certainly suffer
break even	['breik 'iːvn] v. make neither profit nor loss
break off	['breik 'ɔf] v. stop doing sth.
brief	[briːf] n. v. instructions/give instructions; we briefed the new

employee = we told him what to do in his job; -ing n. meeting where sb. is briefed

call off	['kɔːl 'ɔf]	v. decide that sth. which has already been arranged will not now happen, e.g. the meeting was called off
campaign	[kæm'pein]	n. a plan of action for a certain purpose e.g. advertising campaign
cancel	['kænsl]	v. decide that sth. which has already been arranged will not now happen, e.g. cancel a meeting
capacity	[kə pæsiti]	n. production capacity = the amount a factory is able to produce
cautious	['kɔːʃəs]	adj. not taking risks; caution n.
chairman	['tʃɛəmən]	n. person in charge of a meeting; chair a meeting
chart	[tʃɑːt]	n. a sheet of paper with statistical information, e.g. a sales chart
c.i.f.	[ˌsiː ai 'ef]	cost, insurance, freight; the price given includes the cost of the product, insurance, and cost of transport
circumstances	['səːkəmstænsiz]	n. in/under the circumstances = considering the facts
client	['klaiənt]	n. a customer
comment	['kɔment]	v. say sth. about; comment['kɔment] n.
commission	[kə'miʃən]	v. appoint sb. to do sth. for you
commission	[kə'miʃən]	n. money paid to sb. for selling goods
commit oneself	[kə'mit wʌnself]	v. he refused to commit himself = he refused to come to a decision/make his position clear
compensation	[ˌkɔmpən'seiʃən]	n. payment for damage
compete	[kəm'piːt]	v. try to do better than others; competition [kɔmpə'tiʃən] competitor [kəm'petitə] n. competitive [kəm'petitiv] adj.
complication	['kɔmpli'keiʃən]	n. a new difficulty
component	[kəm'pəunənt]	n. part of a complete project
compromise	['kɔmprəmaiz]	n. an agreement which settles a problem in an acceptable way although neither side gets everything it wants
concede	[kən'siːd]	v. concede the point = admit that the other person is right
concentrate on	['kɔnsəntreit ɔn]	v. give all one's attention to
conclude	[kən'kluːd]	v. arrive at an opinion; conclusion [kən'kluːʒən] n. draw a conclusion from the facts
conduct	[kən'dʌkt]	v. conduct a survey = carry out a survey
confidence	['kɔnfidəns]	n. we have confidence in his ability = we trust his ability
confidential	[ˌkɔnfi'denʃəl]	adj. secret; in confidence n.
confirm	[kən'fəːm]	v. remove any doubts
confront	[kən'frʌnt]	v. come face to face with; -ation [ˌkɔnfrən'teiʃən] n.
consequence	['kɔnsikwəns]	n. a result or effect of sth.
consignment	[kən'sainmənt]	n. goods to be delivered
constant	['kɔnstənt]	adj. unchanging
consultant	[kən'sʌltənt]	n. an expert who advises on a particular problem; consult v.
consumer	[kən'sjuːmə]	n. a person who buys/uses goods

content	[kən'tent]	adj. satisfied
context	['kɔntekst]	n. a word out of context = a word written or said without the rest of the sentence
controversial	[ˌkɔntrə'vəːʃəl]	adj. likely to cause disagreement; controversy [kən'trɔvəsi] n.
convenience	[kən'viːnjəns]	n. for the sake of convenience = to make things easier
convinced	[kən'vinst]	adj. sure; of the firm opinion
co-operate	[kəu'ɔpəreit]	v. work together
co-ordinate	[kəu'ɔːdineit]	v. to bring into proper relationship, to bring together effectively
corporation	[ˌkɔːpə'reiʃən]	n. (Am.) limited company
course	[kɔːs]	n. one part of a meal, e.g. soup
create	[kriː'eit]	v. make sth. which did not exist/was not there before
current	['kʌrənt]	adj. current projects = projects going on at the moment
cut	[kʌt]	v. cut production costs = spend less on production; cut down work = do less work; cut out work = stop doing work
deadline	['dedlain]	n. final date by which sth. must be done
definite	['definit]	adj. certain; -ly adv.
delegation	[ˌdeli'geiʃən]	n. group of people acting for a company/government, etc.
deny	[di'nai]	v. say that sth. is not true
depart	[di'pɑːt]	v. leave, go away; -ure [di'pɑːtʃə] n.
deputy	['depjuti]	n. adj. second in command
despatch	[dis'pætʃ]	v. send off
device	[di'vais]	n. sth. designed for a special purpose
diary	['daiəri]	n. book in which daily events are noted
D.C.	['diː'siː]	n. direct current, flow of electricity in which positive and negative poles are always the same, see A.C.
disaster	[di'zɑːstə]	n. terrible misfortune
disclose	[dis'kləuz]	v. make known
discount	['diskaunt]	n. amount of money taken off the full price
disgusted	[dis'gʌstid]	adj. having a violent feeling of dislike
dismiss	[dis'mis]	v. he was dismissed = he was told to leave his job; -al n.
disrupt	[dis'rʌpt]	v. throw into disorder
distribute	[dis'tribjut]	v. give out, send out; distribution n. distributor n.
diversify	[dai'vəːsifai]	enter into new fields, do new types of work; diversification [daiˌvəːsifi'keiʃən] n.
dividend	['dividend]	n. regular payment to sb. who has put money into a business
draft	[drɑːft]	n. v. rough notes; an outline draft of the report = the first written outline of the report
drawback	['drɔːbæk]	n. disadvantage
edge	[edʒ]	n. have the edge over a competitor = have an advantage over a competitor
efficient	[i'fiʃənt]	adj. able to do sth. well, with the minimum waste of work/time; efficiency n.

emphasize [ˈemfəsaiz] v. give special importance to; emphasis [ˈemfəsis] n.

enclose [inˈkləuz] v. I enclose the tickets = I have put the tickets in the envelope

encourage [inˈkʌridʒ] v. give hope; encouraging adj.

entail [inˈteil] v. make necessary

entertain [ˌentəˈtein] v. receive sb. as a guest

entire [inˈtaiə] adj. complete, whole; -ly adv.

equip [iˈkwip] v. supply with articles for a special purpose; -ment n.

essential [iˈsenʃəl] adj. absolutely necessary

establish [iˈstæbliʃ] v. set up; -ed adj.

eventual [iˈventʃul] adj. final, in the end; -ly adv.

evidence [ˈevidəns] n. fact which gives a reason for believing sth.

exaggerate [igˈzædʒəreit] v. say that sth. is more than it really is

exclude [iksˈkluːd] v. leave out

exist [igˈzist] v. be; -ing adj.

expand [iksˈpænd] v. make larger, grow larger; expansion [iksˈpænʃən] n.

extend [iksˈtend] v. make longer; extension [iksˈtenʃən] n.

facility [fəˈsiliti] n. buildings and machines are production facilities, buses and trains are transport facilities

file [fail] n. the SC1 file = the papers concerning the SC1

finance [faiˈnæns] n. money

finance [faiˈnæns] v. supply money for sth; financial adj.

fire brigade [ˈfaiə briˌgeid] n. men who put out fires

force [fɔːs] n. group of people, e.g. labour force, sales force

forecast [ˈfɔːkɑːst] n. v. say what will happen in the future

fork-lift truck [fɔːk lift ˈtrʌk] n. a vehicle (usually electric) which can lift and lower heavy objects on two metal arms

freight [freit] n. v. goods, send goods

furious [ˈfjuəriəs] adj. very angry

gain [gein] v. win

gasolene [ˈgæsəliːn] n. (Am.) petrol

get under way [ˈget ʌndə ˈwei] v. begin

grounds [graundz] n. on the grounds of expense = because of expense

heading [ˈhediŋ] n. words coming before each part of a report to show what follows

hold water [ˈhəuld ˈwɔːtə] v. the argument doesn't hold water = the argument can be shown to be wrong

host [həust] n. sb. who receives a guest

identify [aiˈdentifai] v. recognize

ignore [igˈnɔː] v. take no notice of

imply [imˈplai] v. suggest

impress [imˈpres] v. The Board were impressed by the SC1 = the Board formed a

	favourable opinion of the SC1; impressive adj.
incident	[ˈinsidənt] n. event
indicate	[ˈindikeit] v. show
indiscreet	[indisˈkriːt] adj. not careful in what one says (about secret things)
inevitable	[inˈevitəbl] adj. certain to happen
infringe	[inˈfrindʒ] v. infringe a rule = break a rule (infringe a patent)
initiative	[iˈniʃjətiv] n. on his own initiative = without first getting approval
injunction	[in dʒʌŋʃən] n. written order from a law court
insist on	[inˈsist ɔn] v. I insist on immediate payment = I will accept nothing but immediate payment; he insists on coming = no one can stop him coming
instruct	[inˈstrʌkt] v. tell, order
intervene	[ˌintəˈviːn] v. interrupt, to come between two people who are arguing or fighting
invest	[inˈvest] v. put money into a company; -or n. -ment n.
investigate	[inˈvestigeit] v. examine, inquire into
invoice	[ˈinvɔis] n. v. bill for goods or services supplied
involved in	[inˈvɔlvd in] adj. take part in or become part of
issue	[ˈiʃu] n. question, problem
item	[ˈaitəm] n. item on the agenda = one of a list of questions to be discussed
judgement	[ˈdʒʌdʒmənt] n. ability to decide, make a decision
labour	[ˈleibə] n. work
launch	[lɔːnʃ] v. launch a product = put a product on the market, start selling a product
licensing agreement	[ˈlaisənsiŋ əˌgriːmənt] n. contract/agreement to let another company produce your goods under licence in return for payment
life-cycle	[ˈlaif ˈsaikl] n. (of a product) time during which a product sells well enough to be worth producing and selling
link	[liŋk] n. v. connection
liquidity	[liˈkwiditi] n. availability of cash to make payment, rather than credit on assets e.g. property, equipment etc.
maintain	[meinˈtein] v. keep, look after equipment, buildings
maintain	[meinˈtein] v. hold an opinion
major	[ˈmeidʒə] adj. chief, very important
manoeuvrability	[məˌnuːvrəˈbiliti] n. ability to be moved in a small space
manufacture	[ˌmænjuˈfæktʃə] v. make, produce
mechanism	[ˈmekənizm] n. machine
memo	[ˈmeməu] n. a note sent to another person, usually in the same company. It does not carry an address, greetings etc, like a letter
merchant bank	[ˈməːtʃənt ˈbæŋk] n. trading bank
merely	[ˈmiəli] adv. only
merge	[məːdʒ] v. join together to become one; merger n.

	a joining of two or more companies
mess	[mes] n. state of disorder
minimize	['minimaiz] v. make as small as possible
minute	['minit] n. minutes of a meeting = official written records of what was said at a meeting
motion	['məuʃən] n. a suggestion or proposal to be discussed and voted on at a meeting
moreover	[mɔː'rəuvə] adv. in addition
negotiate	[ni'gəuʃieit] v. discuss, in order to reach an agreement
obliged to	[ə'blaidʒd tu] adj. he was obliged to explain the position = he had to explain the position
obstruct	[əb'strʌkt] v. be in the way, make difficulties; -ive adj.
obtain	[əb'tein] v. get for oneself
occur	[ə'kəː] v. happen
operation	[ˌɔpə'reiʃən] n. activity
outlet	['autlet] n. sales outlet = place where goods are sold to the public, e.g. a shop, an agency
output	['autput] n. amount of production; weekly output of a factory = the quantity produced by the factory in a week
outstanding	[aut'stændiŋ] adj. not yet completed
overlap	[ˌəuvə'læp] v. our duties overlap = our duties are partly the same
overlook	[ˌəuvə'luk] v. fail to see
participate	[pɑː'tisipeit] v. take part in
percentage	[pə'sentidʒ] n. the number per hundred
perform	[pə'fɔːm] v. do; the SC1 performed excellently; -ance n.
persist in	[pə'sist in] v. keep on doing sth; he persisted in arguing with the directors = he kept on arguing with the directors
persuade	[pə'sweid] v. reason with sb; in order to make him do sth.
point	[pɔint] n. fact or idea mentioned in discussion; raise a point = introduce a new thought for consideration
policy	['pɔlisi] n. general aims
policy	['pɔlisi] n. contract of insurance
pollution	[pə'ljuːʃən] n. making one's surroundings dirty
postpone	[pəus'pəun] v. put off to a later date
potential	[pə'tenʃəl] adj. possible
precedent	['presidənt] n. set a precedent = set an example for the future
preliminary	[pri'liminəri] adj. done first as a preparation
premium	['priːmjəm] n. amount paid for insurance
previous	['priːvjəs] adj. earlier
primary	['praiməri] adj. first, most important; primarily adv.
principal	['prinsipl] adj. chief, most important
principle	['prinsipl] n. in principle = in general
prior	['praiə] adj. earlier in time, earlier in order

priority	[prai'ɔriti] n. the greatest importance
proceed	[prə'si:d] v. go forward
process	['prəuses] v. data processing = arranging information usually with a computer
production line	[prə'dʌkʃən lain] n. the men and machinery taking part in production
product line	['prɔdʌkt lain] n. type of product
project	['prodʒekt] n. plan for development
promote	[prə'məut] v. promote greater understanding = work for greater understanding; move up into a better job
propose	[prə'pəuz] v. suggest; proposal n.
prospect	['prɔspekt] n. possibility for the future
protest	['prəutest] n. a strong objection; protest [prə'test] v.
prototype	['prəutəutaip] n. the first model to be developed
publicity	[pʌ'blisiti] n. it was given a lot of publicity = everyone heard or read about it; a publicity agent = sb. paid to organise advertisements
punctual	['pʌŋtʃul] adj. not late, on time
purchase	[pə:tʃəs] v. n. buy; sth. that is bought
put up	['put 'ʌp] v. he put up a proposal = he made a proposal, he put forward a proposal
qualify	['kwɔlifai] v. pass a test; he is a qualified engineer = he has been trained and has passed an examination as an engineer; qualification [ˌkwɔlifi'keiʃən] n.
questionnaire	['kwestʃə'nɛə] n. a list of questions to be answered, used for the purpose of getting information on a subject
quote	[kwəut] v. repeat the exact words sb. has used
quote the price	['kwəut ðə 'prais] v. name the price; quotation [kwəu'teiʃən] n.
radiator	['reidieitə] n. radiator of a car=the part where the water is cooled
ratio	['reiʃiəu] n. cost-price ratio = the relationship between the cost and the price
reaction	[ri:'ækʃən] n. I don't know what his reaction was = I don't know what effect it had on him; react v.
reassure	[ˌri:ə'ʃuə] v. tell sb. that there is no need to worry; reassurance n.
recharge	['ri:'tʃɑ:dʒ] v. recharge a battery = put electricity back into a battery
record	['rekɔ:d] n. a written account of sth; record [ri'kɔ:d] v.
recover	[ri'kʌvə] v. get better get back sth. which was lost; recovery n.
reduce	[ri'dju:s] v. make smaller, make less; reduction [ri 'dʌkʃən] n.
reject	[ri'dʒekt] v. decide against, refuse to accept; rejection n.
relevant	['relivənt] adj. related to the subject under consideration; relevance n.
reluctant	[ri'lʌktənt] adj. not very willing; reluctance n.
rely on	[ri'lai ɔn] v. depend on; reliable adj.
replace	[ri:'pleis] v. we'll have to replace this old machinery = we'll have to buy

	some new machinery to use in place of the old; replacement n.
represent	[ˌrepriˈzent] v. he represents Bellcrest = he acts for Bellcrest; this represents an improvement = this is a sign of improvement; representative adj.
reputation	[ˌrepjuˈteiʃən] n. they have a good reputation = it is the general opinion that they are good; reputable [ˈrepjutəbl] adj.
require	[riˈkwaiə] v. need; requirement n.
research	[riˈsəːtʃ] n. study of a subject so as to discover new facts
resign	[riˈzain] v. give up one's job; resignation [ˌrezigˈneiʃən] n. a letter of resignation
resistor	[riˈzistə] n. a means of changing a flow of electricity into heat
resolve	[ˌriˈzolv] v. decide resolve an argument = put an end to the argument; resolution [ˌrezəˈljuːʃən] n. formal decision reached at a meeting
resources	[riˈzɔːsiz] n. money, supplies etc. available for use
responsible	[risˈpɔnsəbl] adj. he is responsible for that = it is his duty to do that; responsibility [risˈpɔnsəˈbiliti] n. a position of responsibility = a position where decisions must be taken
retain	[riˈtein] v. keep; retention [riˈtenʃən] n.
returns	[riˈtəːnz] n. profit
reveal	[riˈviːl] v. he revealed the secret = he let the secret be known
review	[riˈvjuː] v. n. examine, look carefully at
revise	[riˈvaiz] v. change so as to improve, reconsider; revision [riˈviʒən] n.
revive	[riˈvaiv] v. bring back into use; revival n.
rig up	[ˈrig ˈʌp] v. you must rig up a demonstration = you must arrange a demonstration
rival	[ˈraivl] n. a person or company that wants to do better than you; rivalry n.
rumour	[ˈruːmə] n. there have been rumours about it = people have been saying things about it but nobody knows if these things are true
run down	[ˈrʌn ˈdaun] v. run down production = produce less
sarcastic	[sɑːˈkæstik] adj. speaking in a cruel way sarcasm [ˈsɑːkæzm] n. cruelly or bitterly worded, in a bitter or cruel voice
sceptical	[ˈskeptikl] adj. finding it difficult to believe; scepticism [ˈskeptisizm] n.
scope	[skəup] n. scope for discussion = opportunity for discussion; it is outside the scope of the report = it is not inside the area of the report
screen	[skriːn] n. an object used for showing photographs, e.g. a film screen
second	[ˈsekənd] v. second a motion = allow your name to be used to show that you support the suggestion put forward by another, to speak in favour of the suggestion put forward
second-rate	[ˈsekəndˈreit] adj. not the best, not first class
sector	[ˈsektə] n. an area of industry, e.g. private vehicle sector
security	[siˈkjuəriti] n. safety; the security officer = person in charge of safety arrangements

select	[si'lekt] v. choose; selection [si'lekʃən] n.
senior	['si:njə] adj. a senior member of staff = one who holds a high position
series	['siəri:z] n. a number of things each related to the one before, e.g. 1, 2, 3, 4 is a series of numbers
setback	['setbæk] n. a difficulty or problem which stops progress
share	[ʃɛə] n. he has shares in oil = he has put money into an oil company and gets part of the profits; shareholder n.
site	[sait] n. place where sth. will be built
soak	[səuk] v. make very wet
sole	[səul] adj. only
solve	[sɔlv] v. find an answer; solution [sə'lu:ʃən] n.
sound	[saund] adj. safe, not taking risks
source	[sɔ:s] n. place where sth. originates
specifications	[ˌspesifi'keiʃənz] n. detailed plan for the design of sth.
staff	[stɑ:f] n. employees working for a company
stage	[steidʒ] n. at this stage = now, at this time in the development
state	[steit] v. say, declare; -ment n.
stock	[stɔk] n. goods held in store stocktake ['stɔkˌteik] v. check the stock
strain	[strein] v. overstretch; strain the resources = do sth. for which the resources are hardly enough
stress	[stres] v. give importance to
strict	[strikt] adj. clear and exact
sub-contract	[ˌsʌb'kɔntrækt] n. a contract with a company for carrying out work which that company has already contracted to do; sub-contract [ˌsʌbkən'trækt] v.
subject to	['sʌbdʒikt tu] prep. dependent on
submit	[səb'mit] v. submit a report = put a report forward to be discussed
subsidiary	[səb'sidjəri] adj. n. a subsidiary company is controlled by another company.
sufficient	[sə'fiʃənt] adj. enough
summary	['sʌməri] n. a short report which includes only the most important things
supplement	['sʌplimənt] n. addition to sth.
surge diverter	['sə:dʒ dai'və:tə] n. a device for protecting electrical equipment from a sudden flow of electricity
survey	['sə:vei] n. a systematic enquiry; survey [sə:'vei] v.
suspend	[səs'pend] v. stop doing sth. for the moment
switch	[switʃ] v. n. change
tackle	[tækl] v. tackle a problem = deal with a problem
take aback	['teik ə'bæk] v. he was taken aback = he was very surprised
take over	['teik 'əuvə] v. get control of; takeover ['teikˌəuvə] n.
term	[tə:m] n. length of time; long-term profits = profits received after a long time
terminate	['tə:mineit] v. finish

terms	[tə:mz] n. in terms of = with regard to; terms of reference = exact description of a subject to be dealt with; terms of payment = conditions of payment
tie down	['tai 'daun] v. tie sb. down = limit his freedom of action, make him promise to do sth.
tough	[tʌf] adj. hard to cut and eat
transfer	[træns'fə:] v. change, move; transfer ['trænsfə:] n.
turn down	['tə:n 'daun] v. turn down an offer = refuse an offer
tyre	[taiə] n. rubber air-filled covering on a car wheel
undertake	[ˌʌndə'teik] v. agree to do, start work on
underwrite	['ʌndərait] v. agree to pay the cost of insurance claims; -r n.
utmost	['ʌtməust] adj. n. the greatest possible
vacant	['veikənt] adj. empty; fill a vacancy = appoint someone to a job
vary	['vɛəri] v. change, be different; variable adj.
vehicle	['vi:ikl] n. means of transport by road, e.g. car, bus
vital	['vaitl] adj. of the greatest importance
volume	['vɔljum] n. amount
warehouse	['wɛəhaus] n. a building for storing goods
water	['wɔ:tə] see – 'hold water'
whereas	[wɛər'æz] conj. on the other hand
whole-hearted	['həul'hɑ:tid] adj. he gave me his whole-hearted support; -ly adv.
windscreen	['windskri:n] n. front window of a car
withdraw	[wið'drɔ:] v. withdraw a loan = take away a loan; -al n.
within	[wi'ðin] prep. prep. within a week = before the end of seven days
worthwhile	['wə:θ'wail] adj. worth doing